ENCOUNTERING THE SPIRIT

TRADITIONS OF CHRISTIAN SPIRITUALITY SERIES

ENCOUNTERING THE SPIRIT

The Charismatic Tradition

Mark J. Cartledge

SERIES EDITOR:
Philip Sheldrake

DARTON·LONGMAN + TODD

First published in 2006 by
Darton, Longman and Todd Ltd
1 Spencer Court
140–142 Wandsworth High Street
London SW18 4JJ

ISBN-10: 0-232-52615-X
ISBN-13: 978-0-232-52615-8

A catalogue record for this book is available from the British Library.

Unless otherwise stated, the Scripture quotations in this publication are taken
from the Holy Bible, New International Version, Copyright © 1973, 1978, 1984
by International Bible Society.

Typeset by YHT Ltd, London
Printed and bound in Great Britain by CPI Bath

Over the course of my life it has been my privilege to have two elder twin sisters, Valerie and Julie. They were my earliest friends and supporters and they continue to be so to this day. I wish to dedicate this book to both of them with deep heartfelt appreciation for all they are in my life. I look forward to many more years of mutual love and affection and rejoice in the gift of a family.

CONTENTS

PREFACE TO THE SERIES

Nowadays, in the Western world, there is a widespread hunger for spirituality in all its forms. This is not confined to traditional religious people, let alone to regular churchgoers. The desire for resources to sustain the spiritual quest has led many people to seek wisdom in unfamiliar places. Some have turned to cultures other than their own. The fascination with Native American or Aboriginal Australian spiritualities is a case in point. Other people have been attracted by the religions of India and Tibet or the Jewish Kabbalah and Sufi mysticism. One problem is that, in comparison to other religions, Christianity is not always associated in people's minds with 'spirituality'. The exceptions are a few figures from the past who have achieved almost cult status such as Hildegard of Bingen or Meister Eckhart. This is a great pity, for Christianity East and West over two thousand years has given birth to an immense range of spiritual wisdom. Many traditions continue to be active today. Others that were forgotten are being rediscovered and reinterpreted.

It is a long time since an extended series of introductions to Christian spiritual traditions has been available in English. Given the present climate, it is an opportune moment for a new series which will help more people to be aware of the great spiritual riches available within the Christian traditions.

The overall purpose of the series is to make selected spiritual traditions available to a contemporary readership. The books seek to provide accurate and balanced historical and thematic treatments of their subjects. The authors are also conscious of the need to make connections with contemporary experience and values without being artificial or reducing a tradition to one dimension. The authors are well versed in reliable scholarship about the traditions they describe. However, their intention is that the books should be fresh in style and accessible to the general reader.

One problem that such a series inevitably faces is the word 'spirituality'. For example, it is increasingly used beyond religious circles and does not necessarily imply a faith tradition. Again, it could mean substantially different things for a Christian and a Buddhist. Within Christianity itself, the word in its modern sense is relatively recent. The reality that it stands for differs subtly in the different contexts of time and place. Historically, 'spirituality' covers a breadth of human experience and a wide range of values and practices.

No single definition of 'spirituality' has been imposed on the authors in this series. Yet, despite the breadth of the series there is a sense of a common core in the writers themselves and in the traditions they describe. All Christian spiritual traditions have their source in three things. First, while drawing on ordinary experience and even religious insights from elsewhere, Christian spiritualities are rooted in the Scriptures and particularly in the Gospels. Second, spiritual traditions are not derived from abstract theory but from attempts to live out gospel values in a positive yet critical way within specific historical and cultural contexts. Third, the experiences and insights of individuals and groups are not isolated but are related to the wider Christian tradition of beliefs, practices and community life. From a Christian perspective, spirituality is not just concerned with prayer or even with narrowly religious activities. It concerns the whole of human life, viewed in terms of a conscious relationship with God, in Jesus Christ, through the indwelling of the Holy Spirit and within a community of believers.

The series as a whole includes traditions that probably would not have appeared twenty years ago. The authors themselves have been encouraged to challenge, where appropriate, inaccurate assumptions about their particular tradition. While conscious of their own biases, authors have none the less sought to correct the imbalances of the past. Previous understandings of what is mainstream or 'orthodox' sometimes need to be questioned. People or practices that became marginal demand to be re-examined. Studies of spirituality in the past frequently underestimated or ignored the role of women. Sometimes the treatments of spiritual traditions were culturally one-sided because they were written from an uncritical Western European or North Atlantic perspective.

However, any series is necessarily selective. It cannot hope to do full justice to the extraordinary variety of Christian spiritual traditions. The principles of selection are inevitably open to question. I hope that an appropriate balance has been maintained between a sense of the likely readership on the one hand and the dangers of narrowness on the other. In the end, choices had to be made and the result is inevitably weighted in favour of traditions that have achieved 'classic' status or which seem to capture the contemporary imagination. Within these limits, I trust that the series will offer a reasonably balanced account of what the Christian spiritual tradition has to offer.

As editor of the series I would like to thank all the authors who agreed to contribute and for the stimulating conversations and correspondence that sometimes resulted. I am especially grateful for the high quality of their work which made my task so much easier. Editing such a series is a complex undertaking. I have worked closely throughout with the editorial team of Darton, Longman and Todd and Robert Ellsberg of Orbis Books. I am immensely grateful to them for their friendly support and judicious advice. Without them this series would never have come together.

PHILIP SHELDRAKE
University of Durham

ACKNOWLEDGEMENTS

It is inevitable that the writing of a book incurs a variety of debts. A number of these are worthy of mention.

I would like to thank Philip Sheldrake for inviting me to write this book and Darton, Longman & Todd, and especially Brendan Walsh, Sandy Waldron and Helen Porter, for enabling its publication. I hope that it will be a fitting addition to the series.

I would like to express my appreciation to Laura Jarvis who provided some research assistance during the early part of the project and to Neil Hudson for kindly reading my first draft and making insightful comments. Ian Randall sent me a pre-publication copy of his text on the Evangelical tradition in the same series and this has proved an invaluable resource, so to him I express my gratitude for his thoughtfulness.

My wife and daughter, Joan and Rebekah, are, as always, a source of love and support. I am grateful for their patience once again as I work on yet another project!

I have been writing on the subject of Pentecostal and Charismatic theology for almost twenty years, so it is inevitable that I have reused some earlier material, even if it has been reworked for the purposes of this book. I am therefore grateful to the following publishers for the reproduction of this material from previously published work.

Reprinted by permission of Sage Publications Ltd:

'Charismatic Prophecy: A Definition and Description', *Journal of Pentecostal Theology* 5 (1994), pp. 81–122, © Sage Publications Ltd, 1994.

'Practical Theology and Charismatic Spirituality: Dialectics in the Spirit', *Journal of Pentecostal Theology* 10.2 (2002), pp. 107–124, © Sage Publications Ltd, 2002.

Reprinted by permission of Paternoster Press (Authentic Media Ltd):

Practical Theology: Charismatic and Empirical Perspectives (Carlisle: Paternoster, monograph series: *Studies in Pentecostal and Charismatic Issues*, 2003), pp. 18–20, 24–26, © Authentic Media Ltd, 2003.

In addition, I have sought copyright permission to use the words from two contemporary songs in both the UK and USA. Permission has gratefully been received for the following songs:

'All the glory (My heart is full of admiration)', Graham Kendrick © 1991 Make Way Music, PO Box 320, Tunbridge Wells, Kent, TN2 9DE,
www.grahamkendrick.co.uk; administered by Music Services Inc. in the USA, www.musicservices.org.

'I worship you', Carl Tuttle © 1982 Shadow Spring Music; administered by CopyCare, PO Box 77, Hailsham BN27 3EF, music@copycare.com in the UK, and by Music Services Inc. in the USA, www.musicservices.org.

INTRODUCTION

The concept of spirituality has become increasingly important within the vocabulary of Christianity in recent years. But it also has wider appeal and 'spirituality' can be used as an imprecise category appearing to contain all or nothing. The Traditions of Christian Spirituality series enables the concept of spirituality to be used in relation to Christianity by giving it clear traditions of thought. That is, the concept is put to service in relation to specific ecclesial and theological frameworks, thus enabling readers to understand its contours in relation to the main expressions of Christianity. These expressions have been informed by mystical and spiritual sources in the Christian tradition. However, an account of a spiritual tradition which pays particular attention to the person and work of the Holy Spirit is still lacking. This volume is intended to fill that gap.

In the history of the Church there have been key individuals and indeed movements that have stressed the person and work of the Holy Spirit. However, from time to time, the person of the Spirit has been made subordinate to the institutional order (ministerial orders and/or sacraments), or indeed to other persons of the Trinity, thus eclipsing his significance for both theology and the Christian life. At other times there has been such an emphasis on the work of the Spirit that other features of belief and practice have been neglected. With the emergence of the Pentecostal movement in the twentieth century there has been an explosion in attendance to the nature of the Spirit and his work in the Church and the world. This book reflects this renewed

attention and offers a reflection on what I have called
'charismatic spirituality'.

The central motif of the charismatic tradition is the
'encounter with the Spirit' both corporately within the worshipping life of the Church and individually through personal
devotion and ongoing work and witness in the world. This
book uses this key motif to define charismatic spirituality
and to trace the evidence for the charismatic tradition
throughout the history of the Church. The horizon of study is
largely contemporary, especially because the tradition has
become so evident in recent history, but it draws on historical
material at various points along the way. In doing so, one of
the key contentions of this study is supported, namely: that
charismatic spirituality is not new or recent. Rather, it has
been a feature of Christianity from the earliest days, even if
aspects of it have been marginalised and ignored at various
points in history.

In its recent history the charismatic tradition has been
associated with the populist Pentecostal and Charismatic
renewal movements of the twentieth century. These movements have become numerically significant with an estimated
500 million adherents globally. In addition, the theology
associated with these movements has become increasingly
mature and the volume of academic material now published
is a tribute to its life and health. It is hoped that this present
volume, while introducing the tradition to those unfamiliar
with it, might also contribute to the scholarship in the field.

This book begins with two foundational or contextual
chapters. The first chapter defines the nature of charismatic
spirituality, outlines the twentieth-century history of the
Pentecostal and Charismatic movements, and gives a *theological* context by means of two concepts. The first is the
concept of 'process' and indicates the route or journey via
which participants travel on the charismatic journey. The
second concept is 'framework' and gives a structure to the
beliefs, symbols and action of those engaged in the process.
Both these concepts are different ways at looking at the same

reality and they are therefore complementary. They should be held together, although on occasion one will serve the description better and at other times the other one will do so. The second chapter provides a broad *historical* context and traces important persons and movements throughout church history prior to the twentieth century. These traditions are significantly influenced by 'encounters with the Spirit' and they illustrate aspects of both the process and framework.

On the basis of these two chapters there are four thematic chapters that follow. These chapters pick up dimensions of the charismatic tradition that are significant for under-standing the spirituality: praise and worship, inspired speech, the sanctified life and empowered kingdom witness. These are interrelated themes that appear both in the con-temporary expressions of the tradition and in various ways throughout church history. Finally, there is what might be called a co-ordinating chapter to complete the account. It is suggested that these four thematic chapters need to be held together, and whilst this can be done by means of a process and framework, recent theological reflection has turned to theological hermeneutics in order to do this, namely the community of interpreters. It is the church community, however defined, that enables the contemporary expression to be interpreted and re-interpreted in the light of different and changing contexts. Therefore it seems only appropriate that the nature of such interpretation be described in order to complete this introduction to the spiritual tradition.

The authentic charismatic tradition displays a commitment to relate all its thinking to the canon of Scripture as the ultimate witness to and criterion for life in the Spirit. In the 'spirit' of this tradition, I have introduced the thematic and final chapters with a brief summary of biblical material relevant to the subject. It is intended that this should provide an important entry point into the subject areas, as well as enabling comparisons with the biblical material to be made. To do so does not imply that this material belongs solely or exclusively to the tradition, or that this tradition necessarily interprets it better than others, but to indicate its importance. Indeed, one of the contentions of this study is to suggest that the charismatic tradition, far from being isolated, is always played alongside other traditions to a greater or lesser extent. It is hoped that this study will provide sufficient evidence for such a claim. To complete this book, a conclusion summarises the main points, offers a brief assessment of the tradition and quotes an invocation addressed to the Spirit recorded from an Eastern Father of the Church. This invocation not only demonstrates my central thesis but also reflects the central motif of the spirituality and invites participation and worship.

Before I continue, it is necessary to comment on the terminology that I have already started to use in relation to the subject area. The terms 'Pentecostal' and 'Charismatic' are often used interchangeably to refer to denominations, experiential phenomena or a particular kind of theology. I shall use the terms 'Pentecostal' and 'Pentecostalism' to refer to the denominations and movement that emerged during the first half of the twentieth century, normally classified as 'classical Pentecostals'. I recognise that this term is also used as an overarching category for the global phenomenon of 'Pentecostalism', but that is not my usage here. The term 'charismatic' (lower case 'c') will be used in conjunction with the other terms 'spirituality' and 'tradition' and is the focus of this book, while 'Charismatic/s' (upper case 'C') will be used alongside 'movement' or 'Christianity' to refer to the mainstream renewal and New Church movements emerging from the 1960s, or persons identified by these expressions. I shall comment further on these terms in the next chapter.

1. CHARISMATIC SPIRITUALITY

Introduction

The phrase 'encountering the Spirit' encapsulates the essence of charismatic spirituality. All forms of Christian spirituality give an account of the workings of the persons of the Trinity and it is the relationship between the Holy Spirit and the human spirit which gives rise to the notion of spirituality. However, the ways in which the Holy Spirit is located theologically within the different traditions vary enormously. There are some forms of spirituality that are so ordered that spontaneous workings of the Spirit would be regarded as quite improper and indeed impossible. Charismatic spirituality, on the contrary, regards the work of the Spirit to be free and spontaneous as well as, to some extent, patterned and predictable. It is this openness to the workings of the Spirit in ways that might be regarded as 'enthusiastic' as well as mundane that marks out the charismatic spiritual tradition. It is also a spirituality that can be seen within a variety of other spiritual traditions. It has its roots in the Charismatic movements throughout the history of the Church, but especially the Pentecostal movement of the twentieth century. Since the 1960s this particular form of spirituality has travelled widely and has been incorporated within mainstream Protestant and Roman Catholic denominations as well as Eastern Orthodoxy in a much more limited way. New churches have also emerged seeking to build different forms of church structures around a charismatically orientated spirituality.

This chapter aims to set the scene by describing the main

contours of Pentecostal and charismatic spirituality as it has been displayed throughout key movements and people. It will start with the Pentecostal movement and the emergence of the Pentecostal denominations before considering the emergence of the Charismatic movement. I shall also describe my own particular contribution to the discussion by defining charismatic spirituality in terms of the concepts of process and framework before identifying a set of key themes that will be used to paint a portrait of the spirituality. The process and framework provide a *theological* context for the themes that will be treated in more depth, even as chapter 2 provides an *historical* context of the charismatic tradition in church history. Both contexts are important for understanding how the themes are located within the tradition.

Twentieth-century Pentecostal and Charismatic Movements

Pentecostalism in the twentieth century obtains its identity by associating itself with the narrative of the Acts of the Apostles and especially the second chapter of that book. There the disciples are gathered together in one place waiting for the gift of the Holy Spirit, which is promised by Jesus after his ascension to the Father. In the narrative the disciples are suddenly overcome by the presence of the Holy Spirit likened to a mighty wind filling the room and anointing each with his presence, represented by tongues of fire resting upon them. The disciples subsequently speak in different languages and are understood by their hearers to be uttering inspired praise. These disciples are interpreted by Pentecostals to be empowered for witness and the events of the rest of the book of Acts display the Church continuing the ministry of the Messiah, the anointed one, as she is also anointed by the Spirit for works of service. The Acts of the Apostles therefore provides the basis for the life of the Church today because the Holy Spirit is the same Spirit and the Church is in continuity with the anointed ministry of the early Church.

Walter J. Hollenweger, the foremost historical theologian of these movements, has described the oral and African roots of American Pentecostalism as mediated via African American slave religion with its roots in African Traditional Religion.[1] From this background the early Pentecostal movements had their cultural identity within oral and non-Western cultural contexts.[2] This is significant for theology because the primary ways of expressing beliefs are non-literary. Therefore, church liturgies are not written down but oral and understood implicitly. Theology is expressed through testimonies and songs, maximum participation is expected in worship and prayer settings, dreams and visions are the means of receiving prophecy, and the mind/body relationship is understood holistically such that healing and dancing and other physical expressions are affirmed and expected.[3]

The historical figures that signal the emergence of this understanding in the Pentecostal tradition begin with Charles Fox Parham, who in 1900 founded the 'Bethel Bible School' in Topeka, Kansas in the USA. Parham was a Holiness preacher who was searching for a theology of baptism in the Holy Spirit and decided that the biblical evidence for such an encounter with the Spirit was 'speaking in other tongues'. At a watchnight service on 31 December 1900, Parham and his students prayed for this experience and the meeting carried on into the next day. Agnes N. Ozman was prayed for by Parham on 1 January at 11 p.m. and received the baptism in the Holy Spirit evidenced by speaking in tongues.[4] It was reported that she had spoken an unlearned Chinese language. Within a short period Parham and the rest of the students at the Bible School had also spoken in other tongues and Parham had begun to preach about this blessing. Parham applied this experience to missionary work and taught that missionaries need not learn the foreign language of the mission field but could receive it by supernatural means. This view was an early Pentecostal understanding that had to be modified in the light of subsequent missionary experience. Parham, as an itinerant preacher, moved around the USA expounding his teaching and by 1905 had moved to Houston, Texas.

William Seymour was an African American itinerant preacher whom Parham allowed to 'listen in' on the classes, although he was technically employed as a caretaker at the school. He moved to Los Angeles and gathered a small group of Christians at 214 North Bonnie Brae Street to worship and pray. The fire of Pentecost landed on 9 April 1906, a date that is etched in the consciousness of many Pentecostals even today. It is the date associated with the modern-day revival of Pentecost. The group began to grow rapidly and eventually moved to 312 Azusa Street where the full-blown revival continued for three and half years. Seymour was undoubtedly indebted to Parham and the message of baptism in the Spirit, as evidenced by speaking in other tongues, was propagated as the distinctive theological doctrine of the new movement.

From the revival in Los Angeles the message and experience of modern Pentecost spread throughout the USA and beyond. Thomas Ball Barrett visited the USA in 1905 and experienced for himself this encounter with the Spirit. When he returned to Norway he preached the Pentecostal message and revivals began to be established there. Alexander A. Boddy, a Church of England priest working in Sunderland, visited Barrett in 1907 and received the baptism in the Spirit and nine months later also received the gift of speaking in other tongues. Between the years of 1908 and 1914 Boddy organised what came to be known as the 'Sunderland Conventions', promoting the Pentecostal experience and held each year on the feast of Pentecost, known in Anglican circles as 'Whitsuntide'. Conference material and information, including testimonies and sermons, were published in the magazine entitled *Confidence*. From these meetings the British Pentecostal movement emerged to be associated with the names of William Hutchinson, D.P. Williams, George Jeffreys, Nelson Parr and Donald Gee.

As the twentieth century progressed the Pentecostal experience and doctrine was enshrined within denominational

structures as Holiness churches began to become pentecos-
talised. Thus in the USA a number of Pentecostal denominations emerged: for example, the Assemblies of God, the
Church of God (Tennessee) and the Four Square Gospel
Church. In the UK there emerged three main denominations:
the Assemblies of God, Elim and the Apostolic Church
(Wales). Pentecostal denominations proliferated throughout
the twentieth century and they have given rise to new and
different ecclesial structures. In the 1960s and 1970s the
'House Churches', which are today referred to as the 'New
Churches' emerged in the UK.[5] In addition, the spirituality
associated with this particular tradition became integrated
within other more traditional or so-called mainstream
churches.

Dennis Bennett, a priest in the Episcopal Church of the
United States of America (ECUSA), experienced the baptism
in the Spirit evidenced by speaking in tongues in 1959/60 and
was forced to resign his position at a church in Van Nuys,
California. He subsequently worked elsewhere in ECUSA and
'renewal', as it was called, entered into these other churches.
In 1964, an assistant priest, Michael Harper, working at the
famous All Souls Church, Langham Place in London, also
received this encounter with the Spirit and felt constrained to
leave that ministry in order to found a vehicle for charismatic
renewal called the Fountain Trust. This trust published a
magazine to promote its ideas called *Renewal* in 1965; and it
even published an academic journal for a time entitled
Theological Renewal (1975–1983), edited by the famous
renewal theologian of the period, Thomas A. Smail. It was in
1967 that the charismatic renewal also influenced Roman
Catholics and was associated with the University of Notre
Dame and a student parish church of Michigan State University in the USA. From these beginnings charismatic
renewal has influenced many Protestant and Roman Catholic
groups and has even had some influence on Eastern Orthodoxy, although by comparison this influence is extremely
minor.

In most recent church history the influence of the late American evangelical church leader John Wimber must also be noted. He founded the Vineyard denomination and rose to prominence in the UK in the early 1980s when the then famous Anglican evangelist David Watson invited him to visit and conduct a number of meetings. His particular emphasis was upon prophecy, words of knowledge, evangelism and healing as signs of the in-breaking of the kingdom of God. This teaching has become very influential and to some extent superseded the importance of the earlier Pentecostal teaching of baptism of the Spirit and speaking in tongues that the early Charismatics adopted. The Vineyard church in Toronto was the home of the so-called 'Toronto Blessing' in the early 1990s and was associated with certain kinds of phenomena as people encountered the Spirit. They included falling over, weeping, laughing, jumping, shaking and dancing. These phenomena, of course, were not new and have been associated with many similar revivalist events in the history of the Church. However, the availability of cheap air travel enabled thousands of visitors to make the pilgrimage to the Toronto Airport Vineyard Church to experience the blessing and to take it home with them. In the UK the New Wine network would be the main vehicle for Wimber's theological legacy within mainline churches and it continues to grow in influence on the Church of England and independent church denominations (e.g. charismatic Baptist and Vineyard).

It is estimated that Pentecostal and charismatic spirituality is embraced by around 500 million people worldwide. Of course, these numbers would include the many and various expressions of Pentecostal and Charismatic Christianity. It has been suggested that these expressions can be classified in terms of three 'waves' of the Spirit. The first wave is the classical Pentecostal denominations, the second wave is the mainline Renewalists, and the third wave is the new independent churches, including the indigenous churches of Africa and Asia as well as the Vineyard denomination. The

'Third Wave' is now referred to as 'Charismatic' or 'Neo-Charismatic' Christianity.[6] There is diversity between these groups in terms of theology and values, and in how they organise their church life. However, common features would unite them and this enables them to be categorised as 'charismatic'. Essential to these features is the emphasis that at the heart of Christianity there is and should be an *encounter with the Holy Spirit*. This encounter is free, spontaneous, dynamic, transformative and should be an ongoing experiential reality within the purposes of God.

Theological Context: Spirituality as Process and Framework

A contemporary model of Pentecostal and charismatic spirituality can be described in terms of the following process, although it may be applied successfully to other forms of Christian spirituality.

The Process: Search-Encounter-Transformation

It could be argued that every expression of Christian spirituality is an indication of a process of searching for God, who once encountered effects change within the life of the searcher, who is then transformed or renewed in order to continue the journey. The search-encounter-transformation sequence is, of course, continuous and demands constant engagement within both corporate and private spiritual devotions. I have often explained this notion to students by asking them to think about church architecture. When they visit a church where do they think the place of encounter with the divine is symbolically expressed? The Catholics either say the altar or the tabernacle (where the host is reserved), the Protestants tend to say the pulpit (where the Word is preached), and the Pentecostals or Charismatics either talk about the band which dominates the platform (locus of praise) or the fact that there are carpets on the floor (making it easier for people who might fall down while encountering the Spirit). Thus the sacrament, the sermon or the praise/prayer ministry is the locus of encounter with God's Spirit. Of course, these symbols are not exclusive, but they are suggestive of where the accent lies. In a typical charismatic worship service, participants are taken through a search-encounter-transformation cycle. This begins with praise, moves to prayer and the ministry of reading and hearing the Scriptures preached, followed by prayer over and for the people via 'altar calls' or ministry times. The outcome of such encounters with the Spirit is transformation of the person in some way (edification, healing, cleansing, empowerment). Of course, these phases overlap and blur into each other, but the basic pattern is clear enough.

Diagrammatically, it can be described in the following way:

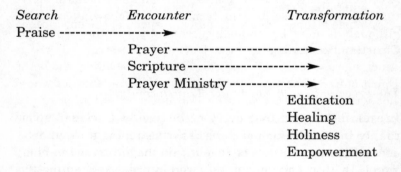

Search	*Encounter*	*Transformation*
Praise --------------------►		
	Prayer --------------------------►	
	Scripture ------------------------►	
	Prayer Ministry ---------------►	
		Edification
		Healing
		Holiness
		Empowerment

From a Christian perspective spirituality concerns not just the process of worship but the life of faith which contains devotional practices and concrete behaviour. Alister E. McGrath defines Christian spirituality in the following way: 'Christian spirituality concerns the quest for a fulfilled and authentic Christian existence, involving the bringing together of the fundamental ideas of Christianity and the whole experience of living on the basis of and within the scope of the Christian faith.'[7] The main components can be seen to comprise a search for the God who is revealed in Christ, and an encounter with this same God by means of the Holy Spirit, which consequently effects change or transformation.[8]

From a very different Christian tradition Mark McIntosh also defines spirituality in terms of search, encounter and transformation. He states:

> [A] discovery of the true 'self' precisely in *encountering* the divine and human other – who allows one neither to rest in a reassuring self-image nor to languish in the prison of a false social construction of oneself...[S]pirituality so conceived is inherently oriented towards discovery, towards new perceptions and new understandings of reality, and hence is intimately related to theology. Perhaps one might think initially in terms of encounter with God as the common ground of spirituality and theology: spirituality being the impression that this encounter makes in the transforming life of people, and theology being the expression that this encounter calls forth as people attempt to understand and speak of the encounter.[9]

Charismatic spirituality is a journey of discovery. There is much more to learn through encountering the other who is the Spirit of God. Of course, Pentecostals and Charismatics would not wish to limit the place of encounter to either praise or prayer, including prayer ministry, but would also see that God is encountered in the preaching of Scripture, in the community of the Church as people have fellowship together and in many events within the life of the worshipping and witnessing Church because the Spirit can and does 'enliven' all things within the kingdom of God. The ways in which all these features can be located within a framework are akin to a 'worldview' and provide a set of lenses through which the world is viewed and by which reality makes sense.

Charismatic spirituality can also be defined in terms of a structure or framework, within which certain themes are displayed.

The Framework: Narrative, Symbols and Praxis

A spirituality defined in this way contains stories through which humans view reality. Narrative is the most characteristic expression of one's spirituality. In addition, symbols express the stories and the answers to basic life questions. These can be artifacts such as buildings, or they can be events such as festivals. Symbols tend to function as boundary markers. They are actions and visible objects that express the spirituality at the deepest level. Finally, spirituality contains praxis, that is, a 'way-of-being-in-the-world'.[10] The real shape of a person's spirituality can be seen in the actions they perform, especially from behaviour that is habitual. Thus, a spirituality literally gives a location from which to view and inhabit the world, enabling purposeful action. Therefore narrative, symbols and praxis interpret the spirituality at every point and the search-encounter-transformation process can be considered in these terms.

The narrative is provided by the narrative structure of Scripture itself, although enlivened by the Spirit as the Church continues to live in the biblical story. In this respect, the narrative structure is similar to those found in other expressions of Christianity, but the difference lies in pneumatology and participation. There is an expectation and experience, which suggests that the God of the Bible is at work in a similar kind of way today.[11] 'The point of Pentecostal spirituality...[is] to experience life as part of a biblical drama of participation in God's history'.[12] This obedient participation is a *via salutis*, a journey of salvation.[13] Historically, this has derived from the locus of Pentecostal and charismatic experience, namely a second crisis spiritual experience subsequent to conversion-initiation called 'baptism in the Spirit' (see chapter 6). Later Charismatics relativised this experience by speaking of more frequent 'encounters' with the Holy Spirit as part of the ongoing life of the believer. Therefore, Charismatics expect God to reveal his glory in worship, to answer prayer, to perform miracles, to speak directly by means of dreams and visions and prophecy. It is presuppositional to the Pentecostal and charismatic narrative. God is not absent but deeply present.[14] Even if the end of worship is indeed the worship of God, Charismatics expect to experience 'something' of the divine life in the Church because of the sheer graciousness of God.[15] God loves to give himself to his people!

The symbolic world of Charismatics is also shaped by this overarching Christian narrative. Until the late twentieth century, Pentecostals have been the poor relations in the Church. This is still the case in most parts of the world. As such, they could not afford to build enormous edifices that showed how powerful God is. Instead, they had a 'baptism in the Spirit' and spoke in strange tongues, otherwise known as glossolalia.[16] Speaking in tongues is a key symbol for Charismatics because it is the 'cathedral of the poor'.[17] You can speak in tongues anywhere. It does not locate you. Indeed, it becomes a kind of universal language, which is not tied to privilege, power and status. It demonstrates the power of God in the weakness of humanity. It enables a person to identify with a particular group and yet to retain individuality. There are other embodied symbols, often embedded in rituals, such as falling over under the power of the Holy Spirit, or crying or laughing in worship.[18] Indeed, these symbols give expression to one of the deepest domains of personal knowledge: the human emotions. The Pentecostal and charismatic emphasis upon right affections before God and one's neighbour are expressed by means of these key symbols as well as social justice issues.[19]

The praxis of Charismatics can be seen in an enthusiasm for prayer with others. It is the primary theological activity of Pentecostals and Charismatics.[20] It appeals to the intuitive and extrovert: prayer is something to be encountered with others, as well as the Spirit.[21] The way of being in the world is therefore socially expressed prayer. Life is so imbued with the presence of God that prayer becomes a habit. This is a habit formed 'in the Spirit' and received 'through the Spirit'.

Praying in tongues is as natural to many charismatic Christians as any other kinds of prayer. In the various ecclesial traditions, the evidence of prayer ministry teams displays this concern for prayer that is expectant of transformation.[22] So, people express care for one another by praying for each other. The expectation is that God answers prayer in the lives of believers and the world in which we all live. The kingdom of God has broken into this present age with the coming of Christ and the foretaste of this kingdom is opened up by the end-time Spirit.

These three features interpenetrate and are always present to some extent within expressions of the spirituality, giving it structure and shape. Here is a convenient way to envisage it:

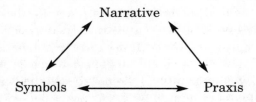

Thus in the telling of the narrative there will also be symbols and actions at work. In the use of symbols, such as the use of carpets in church furnishings, there will be some form of interpretation (relating to the narrative of sacred space), as well as correlating embodied actions ('falling over'). Actions such as 'falling over', or testifying, or singing praise also contain aspects of symbolism (words on a screen) and relate to the narrative.

Main Themes and a Community of Interpreters

So far I have identified a process and a framework for charismatic spirituality. These are really two concepts for describing the reality that I am concerned with. In addition to the process and the framework, one can also describe main themes that are located within both the process and the framework. To use a musical metaphor: these themes provide the different stanzas in the lyrics of the charismatic song. The framework provides the overall shape for the whole song, and the process provides the melody and tempo enabling us to move through the song. To sing the charismatic song one needs to have all three components, although in true charismatic style there are many different ways to improvise in the performance of the song (e.g. classical Pentecostal, Renewalist or Third Wave).

The key themes providing the lyrics for the charismatic song are: praise and worship, inspired speech, holiness and empowered witness in the kingdom of God. Together they form a four-fold thematic typology for identifying the presence of charismatic spirituality, when it is accompanied by the process and framework, however it is 'played' alongside other Christian traditions. Notice how the community of interpreters are at the centre of the ways in which the themes are defined and interpreted. This is because these themes do not emerge from a vacuum but are part and parcel of a worshipping set of communities that seek to embrace and embody this spirituality. How the charismatic tradition will be interpreted in relation to the broader Christian tradition is important and the community of interpreters play a key role in this regard. The following diagram will help to picture the main themes in view, as well as the centrality of the interpretive community.

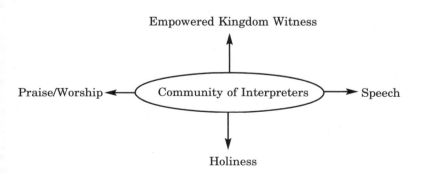

In many respects the kingdom of God is a dominant theme and could be said to encapsulate the others. This category contains the subjects of signs and wonders, healing and miracles, as well as eschatology, witness and baptism in the Spirit. Praise and worship is crucial to charismatic spirituality and is driven by various contemporary approaches to music and hymnody. Speech contains inspired speech such as speaking in tongues, prophecy, prayer, testimony and preaching. Holiness represents the nature of the encounter with the Spirit of God, namely that God's Spirit is Holy. This dimension has been characteristic of the roots of the Pentecostalism with its debt to Wesleyanism, and it is still characteristic of charismatic spirituality. In the chapters that follow, these themes will be explored more deeply. In each theme the central motif of charismatic spirituality, namely 'encountering the Spirit' will be examined in relation to biblical, historical and contemporary sources.

In order to set the historical context, the following chapter will trace the presence of these themes within the history of the Church. In this chapter it is the themes that are in view rather than the process and framework explained here, although one might gain glimpses of these at various points.

2. THE CHARISMATIC TRADITION IN CHURCH HISTORY

Introduction

The aim of this chapter is to *sketch* an important aspect to the central argument of this book, namely, that charismatic spirituality as part of the Christian tradition has been evident throughout the history of the Church.[1] In certain periods of church history it is extremely evident, while at other times it is almost if not totally hidden.[2] Therefore I am suggesting that there is sufficient evidence for 'encounters with the Spirit' and associated theological reflections to indicate the presence of this tradition in Christian spirituality. I do not intend to provide an account of all of the features of charismatic spirituality at every point in history, or indeed to include reference to every historical figure or movement, but to *illustrate* key features in a narrative fashion. This chapter thus provides a necessary historical overview and theological context for the chapters that follow.[3] I begin with the early Church and early Middle Ages, before describing the high Middle Ages and the Reformation and Catholic Reformation period.[4] Finally, I describe the most immediate historical context to twentieth-century Pentecostalism by considering the Post-Reformation period and the Holiness Movement.

The Early Church and the Early Middle Ages

There is significant evidence for charismatic manifestations during the first century, especially documented in the Lukan and Pauline biblical corpus (Luke, Acts, 1 Corinthians). As I shall use biblical material to introduce my main chapters, I simply note the degree of continuity between Old Testament charismatic dimensions and New Testament ones. This is especially the case within the promise-fulfilment trajectory of the canon (e.g. Joel 2 and Acts 2). The biblical narrative forms the background to this church history sketch; and some of these elements are found in the Apostolic Fathers, writing towards the end of the first century and the beginning of the second century CE. Both Clement of Rome and Ignatius of Antioch refer to prophetic gifts, as do the documents we refer to as the *Didache* and the *Shepherd of Hermas*.[5] *Pseudo-Barnabas* also makes reference to prophetic ministry. Prophetic features are continued in the second-century writing of Justin Martyr (*ca* 100–65) and Irenaeus of Lyons (*ca* 130–202). Justin Martyr mentions the reception of charismatic gifts, such as healing, foreknowledge and prophecy, and that miracles have been withdrawn from Israel and given to the Christians. Irenaeus also makes mention of charismatic gifts, including the discernment of spirits and exorcism, as well as the raising of the dead, although he is often associated with the institutionalisation of the Church via orders and sacraments. Both Hippolytus of Rome (d. 236) and Tertullian of Carthage (*ca* 160–225) refer to healing and Tertullian notes exorcisms and gifts of revelation.

In the third century we see the rise of the charismatic movement called the Montanists, led by Montanus, a converted pagan Cybele priest to Christianity, who emphasised prophecy, visions and encounters with angels. Montanus regarded himself as an inspired instrument of the Holy Spirit and allegedly identified himself with the Paraclete promised by Jesus in John's Gospel (ch. 14). He was joined by two women, Maximilla and Priscilla, who made similar prophetic claims. Tertullian is associated with them (from 207 CE) and has been called the first Pentecostal theologian.[6] He certainly defended the movement from attack, regarding it as a form of true spirituality. However, scholars have often been critical of the Montanist movement and the claims that have been made by its adherents. But it is problematic because most of the material comes from anti-Montanist sources, for example, from Hippolytus and Eusebius. It has certainly been the case that Montanism has been revisited by Pentecostal historians and they have been critical of some of the assumptions of traditional scholarship with regard to its interpretation of the movement. In the same century Clement of Alexandria (*ca* 150–215), Origen of Alexandria (*ca* 185–254), Gregory Thaumaturgus of Neocaesatea (*ca* 213–70) and Athanasius' Anthony of the Desert (251?–356) have described healings, exorcisms, prophecies and signs and wonders. Cyprian of Carthage (d. 258) links charismatic gifts with the office of the bishop and thus consolidates the subordination of gifts to offices within the Church.

From the third and moving into the fourth century there continues to be evidence to suggest that aspects of charismatic spirituality are explicit within church life. However, despite his disdain for Montanism, Eusebius (*ca* 260–339) refers to a man called Quadratus who was well known for his prophetic gifts, as well as other 'wonderful works' done through the successors to the apostles. Cyril of Jerusalem (d. 386), while also critical of Gnostic claims to Spirit-inspired knowledge, can affirm the continued manifestation of wisdom, prophecy, exorcism, biblical interpretation, and add the gifts of chastity, virginity and preparation for martyrdom. Cyril is also well known for his explicit linkage of baptism with the reception of the Spirit, thus setting up a debate that successive generations of Christians have entered into. Athanasius (*ca.* 296–373) is famous for his arguments in favour of the full divinity of the Holy Spirit. He is especially noted for expressing the sanctifying work of the Spirit, although he does also make reference to the charismata in the Church of his day. The *Life of St Anthony*, a disputed work of Athanasius, describes the ascetic life of Anthony in the desert and after twenty years of solitude he displays a ministry of signs and wonders, especially the ability to exorcise demons.[7] Finally in this century, John Chrysostom

(347–407), noted for his preaching eloquence, also refers to the holiness that the Spirit gives to believers enabling them to live loving and moral lives. The Spirit is the one who forms character rather than gives charismata and who gives strength to the weak, enabling Christians to live godly lives thus signifying the presence of the Spirit. Significantly, Chrysostom is the first major figure to deny the continuing existence of signs and wonders in the Church, especially speaking in tongues. He regards these as belonging to the first-century Church and having no further validity. This is a view that was to prove influential on subsequent church leaders.

John Cassian (*ca* 365–435) travelled widely and spent a good deal of his life in Syria, Egypt and Constantinople before settling in Marseilles. His writing on the Spirit emphasises the person of the Spirit within a Trinitarian framework. The Spirit combats sin, enables spiritual perfection and ecstatic prayer and allows penetration into the mind of God through the Scriptures and the attainment of spiritual knowledge. The Spirit provides certain virtues to be obtained and gifts received. He categorised the gifts in a three-fold system: (1) gifts of healing; (2) gifts of edification (wisdom, knowledge); and (3) false gifts from demonic sources. True gifts should be used to assist people in the service of God and not admired for their own sake. Therefore love and humility should characterise their usage. He regarded the use of the discernment of spirits as 'a rare and most treasured gift'.

Also in the fourth century but in the East, the Cappadocian Fathers, Basil of Caesarea (b. *ca* 330), his brother Gregory of Nyssa (b. *ca* 335/336) and Gregory of Nazianzen (b. *ca* 330), are significant for their contribution to Trinitarian theology and to the understanding of the Holy Spirit within the Christian life. Through the Church, Basil understood the Spirit as the sanctifier of creation, with each member of the Church being given a gift by the Spirit. These gifts include preaching in the Spirit, the exercising of discernment for those considering ordained ministry and charismata as instruments of virtue. He similarly refers to the Pauline list, including prophecy and healings as gifts enabling the body of Christ to be edified. Gregory of Nyssa, well known for his contribution to the Council of Constantinople (381) and the revised Nicene creed, is a significant Patristic contributor to our understanding of both the Person of the Spirit and the doctrine of the Trinity. In particular, the sacraments as a means of grace and of transformation are to be noted. The anointing of oil (chrismation) is regarded as essential to Christian initiation and bound to the operations of the Spirit. He does, however, refer to gifts of the Spirit and notes 'tongues of angels and prophecy and knowledge and the grace of healing', although he is more concerned with the gift of cleansing of the soul and the ongoing process of sanctification. Gregory of Nazianzus is noted for his Fifth Theological Oration entitled *On the Holy Spirit*. In particular, he enables us to understand that Christians worship God *in* the Spirit and *through* the Spirit (Rom. 8:26). In another sermon, *The Oration on Pentecost*, the Spirit is again associated with the sacrament of baptism, assists Christians in their prayers, indwells them and is essential to the function of a priest. He is aware of the gift of healing and that the Spirit provides a diversity of gifts to Christian disciples.

In the fourth and fifth centuries in the West, there are three notable Fathers, Hilary of Poitiers (*ca* 315–367/68), Ambrose of Milan (b. *ca* 340), and of course Augustine of Hippo (354–430). Hilary was a champion of the divinity of the Spirit in the West around the same time as Athanasius in the East, although he is aware of the limitations of human language when speaking about the divine and will not speculate beyond the words of Scripture. The Spirit sanctifies and enlightens believers; therefore they need to be aware of the gift that God gives them. This means that they should use all the charismata that are available to them, including: wisdom, faith, healing, miracles, prophecy, understanding of doctrine, discernment of spirits, speaking in tongues and the interpretation of tongues. For Ambrose, the Spirit is operative in the reading of Scripture, as the 'mysteries' in Scripture are revealed to the reader. This meant adding to the literal sense an allegorical sense relating to the higher spiritual meaning. His treatise *Of the Holy Spirit* aims to explain this inter- pretation of Scripture. The Spirit is the great dispenser of blessings, of spiritual renewal and the 'ointment of Christ'. Again, we read of the union of the Spirit with the sacraments such that the efficacy of the sacraments is derived from the Spirit. In confirmation the Spirit seals the soul and provides his sevenfold gift. The Spirit illumines the human mind and imparts purity and creativity, leads into truth and lifts believers from earth to heaven.

Augustine stands out as a towering figure among the Church Fathers and his writings have been deeply influential throughout history. He said much about the Holy Spirit, premised on the twin assumptions that the Spirit is God and is a gift of God. He is co-equal with the Father and the Son and proceeds from both, and is of one essence with God and operates inseparably. He used psychological imagery to communicate the unity and the distinctions. This gift given to the Church is in fact equal to the giver of the gift. This gift represents the energizer renewing the moral capacity of people, writing the law of God upon human hearts, forgiving sin and bestowing the love of God upon the Church. The same Spirit assists the believers in their prayers (Rom. 8:26), bestows knowledge and is marked by the bond of peace; previously it was the gift of tongues, which no longer con- tinues within the Church. However, he did believe that cer- tain miracles do continue in the Church and identifies healing as one such example.

Gregory the Great (540–604) is a significant figure in the early history of the Western Church. He regarded the miracle of languages on the Day of Pentecost as signifying that the Church would speak to all nations. This was a reversal of the confusion of Babel. The gifts of the Spirit (Isa. 11:2) provide armour against evil and are the virtues of preachers (1 Cor. 12:8-10). In his writings there are examples of miracles occurring in the lives of his contemporaries. He links such miracles to the work of evangelism and the deepening of the faith of Christians. These gifts, however, can be withdrawn periodically in order to promote humility and guard against error. The most frequently recorded miracles are: healings, raising the dead to life, exorcisms, predictive prophecy and deliverance from danger. Famously, he is credited as the composer of one of the most popular hymns of invocation: *Veni Creator Spiritus*.[8]

The Venerable Bede (*ca* 673–735) from County Durham, England, a Benedictine monk, is regarded as the 'Father of English History'. In his commentary on the Acts of the Apostles, he reflects that on the Day of Pentecost the disciples were filled with the Spirit, and 'burned' and spoke about the Spirit. The Spirit had been poured out on all flesh, regardless of gender, age or social status. In his book on the life of St Cuthbert, he observes how the spiritual gifts are operative in the seventh-century Celtic Church. Cuthbert experienced visions and exercised a healing and prophetic ministry, in addition to exorcisms and an account of the raising of the dead.[9]

In the Eastern Church, Symeon the New Theologian (949–1022), abbot of the monastery of St Mamas, was a well-known charismatic monk and theologian. In his *Ethical Treatises* he describes the baptism in the Spirit. Symeon proposed a second stage in the Christian life, that is a post-baptism event, called Spirit baptism. In this stage there is a greater consciousness of living in Christ, and indeed the Trinity, and of illumination by the Spirit. The theological support for the position is based on Acts 8:14-17. He contends that the Spirit is experienced in his day just as he was in the days of the early Church. This conscious awareness of the Spirit's activity is God's means of deification. However, Symeon does not expect that the gift of tongues will accompany this experience. Rather it is accompanied by the gift of tears, 'an intensified experience of compunction', and visionary experiences of the Trinity as light. He also aligns the fruit of the Spirit with this experience, thus enabling greater obedience and greater zeal. His theology came to doxological expression most clearly in his forty-first hymn, beginning with the words: 'From on high give me your grace, give me your divine Spirit!'[10]

The High Middle Ages

In the High or Late Middle Ages there are a number of significant groups and individuals who display aspects of the charismatic tradition. These include the Cathars, who were radical dualists condemned at Orlean in 1022, for advocating the *consolamentum*, that is, the baptism with fire and the Holy Spirit with the imposition of hands, at which the soul and the spirit were united and the soul passed out of the power of Satan. It was considered to be a moment of cleansing, perfecting and salvation. This theological stance led to persecution for those associated with the movement.

Bernard of Clairvaux (1090–1153) was especially known for his miracles and exorcisms. Bernard taught that the divine can only be known via contemplation not reason. The spiritual life is likened to a journey accompanied by the Holy Spirit who enables union with God. Ecstatic contemplation is a gift of the Spirit, a kiss of participation in the divine life, through which intellect, will and feelings are perfected. To receive this gift of the Spirit, one must renounce fleshly pleasures because the Holy Spirit cannot reside in sinful vessels. Once received the Spirit enables miracles, discernment of spirits and godly virtues.

One of the greatest female mystics of this period in church history was Hildegard of Bingen (1098–1179).[11] She entered a religious community at the age of eight and was eventually made an abbess. She had visions from the age of five, but received a calling to proclaim God's words in the Spirit by means of an ecstatic vision at the age of forty-two. She was taken very seriously as a prophet by the Church and developed an extensive preaching ministry. She also had musical gifts and believed that the Spirit taught the prophets to write psalms and hymns and invent musical instruments to enable praise to be sung. She is reported to have sung in the Spirit, the sound of which was regarded as a 'concert'. For Hildegard the Spirit of God is a creative and re-creative wind or breath, active in the incarnation, the resurrection and baptism. The Spirit is the 'spirit of holiness' able to sanctify the elect who have been touched with the fiery tongues of the Spirit. She regarded her mid-life calling as a personal Pentecost, which is necessary if one is going to manifest divine fruit. The Spirit's work is also linked to the sacramental process of baptism, confirmation and eucharistic participation. Hildegard understands the gifts of the Spirit in pairs: wisdom and understanding, counsel and fortitude, piety and knowledge, which lead to the seventh, fear of the Lord (Isa. 11:2-3). The gifts of the Spirit are numerous and are gifts for service, including the gift of tears, knowledge, the ability to overcome demonic forces and the miraculous.

Richard of St Victor (d. 1173) is known for his writings, especially *De Trinitate*. Richard regards the Trinity as a community in love and the Spirit as the overflow of the love from the Godhead. The Spirit is the creative force in the universe, and the Trinity operates via the Spirit in creation and providence. For Richard, the Spirit is present only to rational creatures, and enables them to confess that Jesus is Lord. Gifts of the Spirit apportioned according to his will include: wisdom, knowledge, faith, healing, miracles, prophecy and the discernment of spirits. Visions and dreams are also possible and these produce ecstasy as divine reality is apprehended.

An important prophetic figure of this period was Joachim of Fiore (*ca* 1130–1202).[12] He had a vision while on a pilgrimage as a young man to the Holy Land and believed that as a result he understood Scripture. His second vision and its contents became the basis of his three main books. On returning to Italy and living in a Cistercian monastery he had another vision of an angel imparting knowledge. He became a Cistercian abbot and encouraged by the Pope (Clement III) wrote out all his prophecies. He is best known for his view of human history in three epochs belonging to the Father, the Son and the Spirit respectively. The present age is the age of the Spirit, a time characterised by the power of the Spirit at work in the Church. In this age new religious orders will be empowered to evangelise all peoples. It will be categorised according to the seven types of Christians (the spiritual Father, contemplative men, learned men, manual labourers, the old and weak, chaste priests and clerics, and the married and their children). At certain points his vision of this age of the Spirit is unclear and open to a variety of interpretations. His followers were persecuted by the Church at the time.

Bonaventure (*ca* 1217–74), a Franciscan friar and theologian, wrote extensively on theology and the spiritual life. This spiritual life is an inner journey upward into the mystery of the triune God. It is a journey in the Spirit until mystical union is obtained. The Spirit's gifts of understanding and wisdom build upon human abilities to enable cognition beyond merely human capacities. By the Spirit the fullness of the special gifts of Christ is given to believers and illumines the intellect and the will. For Bonaventure, the Church was born on the Day of Pentecost when the Spirit was given to the disciples. He describes spiritual gifts from the list of Isaiah 11:2-3 and sees them as given for the purpose of holiness. In addition, he gives attention to prophecy and spiritual ecstasy. In his accounts of the life of Francis of Assisi, he gives descriptions of intense spiritual experiences, drunkenness in the Spirit, revelations, powerful preaching, prophecy and miracles.

The person who is regarded as the greatest philosopher and theologian of this period in the Western Church is Thomas Aquinas (*ca* 1225–74). In the Augustinian tradition he regarded the Spirit as the bond of love within the Godhead and held that this love is placed within us by his grace. The indwelling Spirit forgives sins and justifies, so that the recipient participates in the divine life and is adopted as God's child. Spiritual habits enable Christians to perform supernatural works and express the virtues of faith, hope and love. The seven-fold supernatural endowments of the Spirit also enable a disposition towards the good in a stable ongoing fashion (Isa. 11:2-3). The fruit of the Spirit (Gal. 5:22-3) are also acts of virtue and actions in which humans can delight. Indeed, the summit of the spiritual life is characterised by the beatitudes (Matt. 5:3-10) and these are brought about by the Spirit at work in the human soul. Although the gifts of the Holy Spirit are habits of grace, the charismatic or extraordinary gifts are understood as transitory. The former is directed towards the sanctification of the individual, while the latter is for the good of others. The charismatic graces are categorised as prophecy, speech and action. Prophecy can include all the other gifts of knowledge, speech includes tongues, interpretation (of all kinds of speech) and utterances of wisdom and knowledge, while the action includes healings and miracles. His early biographers recall how his sermons were accompanied by miracles and that during Mass he frequently experienced ecstasy. His spirituality was expressed in hymns, especially *Almum flamen vita Mundi*.[13]

Gregory Palamas (1296–1359) wrote from out of a debate with a Greek-Italian philosopher, Barlaam, regarding the relationship between transcendence and immanence and the human experience of God. Palamas was impressed by the hesychasts (orthodox mystics) who claimed to experience God through their use of the Jesus Prayer. However, he also recognised the force of the transcendentalist argument of Barlaam. In order to mediate between these two opposites, he proposed a middle way. He suggested that while God cannot be known in his essence he can be known via his energies. These energies are not identical to the persons of the Godhead but are possessed and exercised by all three persons. The Holy Spirit works through these energies to deify humanity, thus enabling it to become an instrument of God.

Therefore, there are gifts of the Spirit at work in the Church: healing, miracles, knowledge, wisdom and holiness. In addition, Palamas notes that the gifts of speaking in tongues and interpretation, and words of instruction in response to prayer are still evident in the Church. He also described the possibility that a person so focused in prayer may experience ecstasy, in which a person is seized by the light of the eternal Trinity.

Similarly, Nicholas Cabasilas (*ca* 1320–*ca* 1371) defended the hesychasts, but he stressed the role of the sacraments as the source of spiritual illumination and he did not distinguish between the essence and energies of God. In his works, he argued that mystical union with Christ is mediated via the three 'mysteries' of baptism, chrismation and the eucharist. It is especially through chrismation that Cabasilas regarded the gifts of tongues, prophecy and healing to be conferred alongside godliness, love and sobriety. The fullness of the Christian life, however, is nurtured and sustained in the eucharist, in which the Holy Spirit transforms the elements and God gives himself to his friends, thus transforming them as well.

Reformation and Catholic Reformation Period

The Reformation period was hugely significant for the Church and yet the role of the Holy Spirit was defined in very different ways among the theologians of the time.

Martin Luther (1483–1546), the Augustinian monk turned reformer, is one of the most significant figures in the history of the Church. For Luther, the Spirit brings to the believer the treasure of Christ, enabling him or her to conform to Christ's death and resurrection. The Spirit intercedes on behalf of sinners and sustains them in their *Anfechtung* (inner conflict). Conversion is accompanied by an 'inner witness of the Spirit'. This Spirit works through two divinely instituted external signs, namely the Word of God (spoken, preached or read) and the visible signs of baptism and the

Lord's Supper. For Luther the Spirit speaks through the Scriptures and is the living voice of God. But his commitment to the two signs as means of grace led him to criticise the enthusiasts or 'heavenly prophets' for placing the internal work of the Spirit before the external Word of God. He also accuses them of works' righteousness because of the perfectionist ethic and willingness to be martyred. Luther believed that gifts such as speaking in tongues and (outer) miracles are no longer needed as confirmatory signs of the gospel. His theology of Pentecost is expressed in his 1524 hymn as an outpouring of grace on the believer's mind and heart bringing fervent love and a union in the faith.[14]

The leader of the Swiss reformation, Ulrich Zwingli (1484–1531), was based in Zurich. He is famous for his dispute with Luther at Marburg in 1529 regarding the eucharistic presence of Christ. He believed that the Holy Spirit had come instead of Christ's bodily presence and that the Spirit could be experienced whenever God chooses. Although, like Luther, he believed that the Scriptures are the sole norm for doctrine, he considered that one should consult the mind of the Spirit before interpreting the Bible. Therefore ordinary people can read the Bible and understand what God is saying. The Spirit always agrees with Scripture and is the reliable interpreter of Scripture. Thus the interpreters are imbued with the same Spirit who inspired the biblical texts. In some respects this charismatic biblical hermeneutic made him similar to some of the more radical reformers.

John Calvin (1509–64) was a giant figure of the Continental Reformation and a significant character in Western civilisation. For Calvin, the Spirit is the Spirit of life and orders the cosmos. The image of God in humanity is also dependent on the Word and the work of the Spirit, since the Spirit sustains and is the source of life-giving power. The Spirit bestowed gifts on the people of God, but these have been affected by the Fall, leaving the natural gifts corrupted and supernatural ones withdrawn. But through the Church the cosmic order is being restored via the Spirit, and thus the image of God and right order in society are being restored. Faith, as the work of the Spirit, is the only sign of election. The same Spirit who gives faith is also the one who enables the elect to persevere in it. The Spirit also opens our hearts to the laws of God, making us receptive to Christ in the law. Likewise the Spirit illumines the Scriptures to us, enabling us to discern Christ within the Word. The Word of God is made alive to Christians by the 'internal witness of the Spirit' and this is a testimony to the gospel (not an addition) and is superior to the Church, enthusiasts and reason. It is self-authenticating testimony and certifies biblical truth and the adoption of believers as children of God. Calvin infers that the list of gifts in 1 Corinthians 12:8-10 is for his generation and he understands this list to be partial. However, he regarded the gift of healing as being discontinued, and speaking in tongues as originally a supernatural gift for communicating the gospel, which is no longer required.

The radical reformers were those who rejected both Roman Catholicism and the mainstream Protestant reformers. One of the most notable was Thomas Müntzer (*ca* 1488/9–1525).[15] He separated from Luther in the early 1520s and attempted to establish a pneumatic community of believers imitating the primitive Church. Influenced by the Zwickau prophets ('enthusiasts'), he stressed the importance of the inner word and direct revelation via the Holy Spirit. Unlike the reformers he believed in the powerful working of the Holy Spirit through dramatic experiences. He rejected infant baptism in favour of an inner baptism of the Spirit (based on John 7:38). As a precondition for the baptism, the believer was expected to have been chastised through suffering as a means of preparation and purification. After having received this baptism in the Spirit the believer was able to read the Bible correctly, illuminated by the Spirit, and was free to prophesy and receive revelations via dreams and visions. He also believed that he was living in the last days and that the world was to be renewed totally by the means of the Spirit's reception. His ministry ended through his leadership in the Peasants' War, during which he was captured in 1525 tortured and beheaded.

There are a number of figures associated with the Counter or Catholic Reformation. These are Ignatius of Loyola (1491–1556), John of Avila (1499/1500–69) and John of the Cross (1542–91). I shall focus on Ignatius as indicative of this tradition in relation to the Holy Spirit.

Ignatius of Loyola was a Spanish mystic and founder of the Society of Jesus (Jesuit order) born in Loyola. After a military career he entered a monastery and had a number of visions and wrote his manual, *Spiritual Exercises*. Gathering students together in Paris, he formed the nucleus of a group which became a new order in 1540. Ignatius is a Trinitarian mystic, and wrote of his experiences of all three persons of the Godhead, as well as recognition of their inter-relation. In his intimacy with God he experienced tears, visions, illuminations and various kinds of locutions (God speaking to the soul) as well as other sensations in a mystical state, such as consolation, touches, repose and joy. His mystical experiences of the Spirit are recorded in his *Spiritual Diary* and formed an important part of his contemplative prayer. He and his followers were interrogated frequently by church authorities and accused of being members of the *Alumbrados*, a movement claiming direct and constant inspiration of the Holy Spirit.[16] He was, however, associated with the gift of *loquela*, that is, the gift of mystical speech linked with heavenly music, tones and words, which he heard and spoke. He claims to have heard *loquela* both internally and externally and he prayed for the reception of both kinds of experiences.

Post-Reformation and the Holiness Movement

In the sixteenth to the eighteenth centuries we begin to see greater evidence for the phenomena associated with charismatic spirituality. Thus, Thomas Münster (above) speaks of the inner word of the Spirit, dreams and visions and an imminent Millennium, as well as a baptism in the Spirit.

Ignatius of Loyola (also above) describes visions, tears and *loquela*, that is, sung glossolalia. The seventeenth century brings the Quaker movement and similar phenomena: inner light or word, visions, healings, prophecy and glossolalia. The Camisards also speak of prophecy and glossolalia, and the Jansenists discuss signs and wonders, spiritual dancing, healings, prophecy and glossolalia. In the Moravian Brethren of the eighteenth century we see expressive worship and fervent prayer; and in the First Great Awakening associated with Jonathan Edwards (1703–58) we read of tears, trembling, groans, loud cries and 'religious' noise during encounters with the Spirit. Edwards is noted for his discussion of the discernment of such phenomena in relation to human and divine origins, but he also had a great concern for holiness.[17]

John Wesley (1703–91) is famous for his conversion at Aldersgate in 1738 while listening to a reading of Luther's preface to the epistle to the Romans, as well as his itinerant and open air preaching.[18] Although to some extent tolerant of followers claiming dramatic spiritual experiences, including dreams, visions, healings, revelations and prophecies, he regarded such phenomena as rare and seemed to have little time for 'enthusiasts'.[19] His main contribution to the charismatic tradition, as used by later Christians, is his belief in a post-conversion experience of grace (sometimes called 'perfect love' or 'entire sanctification') enabling the believer to lead a life of devotion to God. This theme will be discussed in more detail in chapter 5.

Around this period Seraphim of Sarov (1759–1833), a Russian Orthodox writer, described the reception of the Spirit and healing. He was a Russian Orthodox monk, who led a solitary life of prayer for most of his ministry but engaged in semi-public ministry for the last eight years of his life. He developed a healing ministry, especially during his *staretz* (elder) period. He demonstrated words of knowledge, whereby he knew the needs of those who came to him before they asked. He based his ministry on the use of the 'Jesus Prayer' and advocated it as a means of peace and purity. He believed that the graces of God are granted to those who love God and their neighbours and have true faith in him. For Seraphim, God can be invoked beyond the eucharist, and God responds to the cry of the heart.

This brings us to the immediate historical context of the Pentecostal movement itself, namely the nineteenth century. In this century there are numerous accounts of charismatic phenomena around the world, from the West of Scotland to Indonesia, South India, the USA and London. The ministry of Edward Irving, a Church of Scotland minister working in Regent's Square, London, is regarded as significant. He is often referred to as the 'morning star of Pentecost', as speaking in tongues and prophecy occurred at his church.[20] But the most important historical antecedent comes from the USA and the Holiness denominations that emerged toward the middle and end of the century. These denominations are inheritors of the Wesleyan Holiness tradition, emphasised revivalism and are directly related to a number of denominations or groups that subsequently became Pentecostal in the twentieth century. They include such groups as the National Holiness Association founded in 1867, the Iowa Holiness Association founded in 1879 and the Church of God (Cleveland, TN) founded in 1886. Indeed many of the early twentieth-century Pentecostal preachers were originally Holiness preachers, such as Charles F. Parham and William Seymour. In the UK, Alexander Boddy was clearly influenced by the holiness teaching via the Keswick Convention, which began in 1875.

Conclusion

At this point we come full circle to our starting point in chapter 1 and the account of classical Pentecostal, Renewalist and Third Wave strands of the tradition. What is important is to understand how this history of the charismatic tradition has demonstrated features of what we now refer to as Pentecostal and charismatic spirituality. In the following chapters I shall describe charismatic spirituality largely from the contemporary period. But I do so with a clear intention that this form of Christian tradition has been expressed throughout history, in and through other Christian traditions. In the twentieth century it came to a particular form of expression by being aligned with the Wesleyan Holiness stream, and subsequently Protestantism more generally as well as with Roman Catholicism. It does not appear to have been well received within Orthodoxy, although there are examples of individuals, as well as churches, moving from Anglicanism or the Vineyard denomination, where the charismatic tradition has been aligned to Orthodoxy, and where it has been 'absorbed'.[21]

3. PRAISE AND WORSHIP

Introduction

Worship is extremely important to Pentecostal and Charismatic Christians. A worship service is the place where people seek the presence of God and from which other kinds of encounter are experienced. It is the place where the glory of the Lord is revealed in power and people are transformed for the sake of the kingdom of God. Of course, worship includes a variety of components: singing, praying, the reading of Scripture and preaching, as well as altar calls or ministry times when people are prayed over for the work of the Holy Spirit to begin or increase in new or deeper ways.[1] It also includes the sacraments of baptism and Holy Communion and other expressions, which are considered to have sacramental qualities, such as foot-washing and speaking in tongues. As Pentecostal churches have become large during the twentieth century, musical accompaniment has become increasingly sophisticated with bands and orchestras in attendance.[2]

Charismatic Christians take their inspiration with regard to praise from the Bible. Indeed, as an aspect of worship, it is evident throughout the canon of Scripture. We find songs of praise from the 'Song of Moses and Miriam' (Exod. 15:1-18), which extols the Lord for the deliverance of Israel from captivity in Egypt, to the roar of the great multitude, the twenty-four elders and four living creatures for salvation, judgement, vengeance and the reign of God with the wedding of the Lamb and his Bride (Rev. 19:1-8). Throughout the canon of Scripture praise and worship surface as the people of God give glory to their creator, redeemer and Lord. There is, however, a concentration of material in the hymn book of the Bible, the Psalter.

King David contributed enormously to the content of praise within the Bible by virtue of the Psalms. The Psalter is full of songs of praise ascribed to him, for example, Psalms 8, 9, 19, 20, 24, 29, 61, 62, 103, 108, 109, 138 and 144. In addition to this material from the Psalter, and indeed to his dancing before the ark in praise (for which he is famous – 2 Sam. 6:14), we also read of certain songs within the biblical narrative. For example, we read of David's song of praise in 2 Samuel 22:2-51, also recorded as Psalm 18, after he had been delivered from his enemies, including Saul. In this song the Lord is designated his rock, fortress and deliverer, refuge, shield and horn of salvation. The Lord is worthy of praise because of his deliverance of David, responding to his prayer for help. In this song we have a glimpse of the imagery used by contemporary Charismatics: the earth trembles, the heavens part and the Lord descends, the brightness of his presence blazes forth, his voice thunders and his enemies are scattered. David is rescued in a powerful way and brought into a spacious place because of the Lord's delight. The righteous one has been spared and rewarded according to his holiness. So the Lord is exalted as the perfect one, and who arms his servants with strength, speed and agility, and safe paths so that his enemies can be pursued and crushed and the victory gained for God's glory. Another example is the song of thanksgiving recorded in 1 Chronicles 16:8-22 (and found as Ps. 105:1-15), which includes such ideas as praise for God's actions, seeking the Lord's face, remembrance of wonders and judgements and God's faithfulness to the covenant.

Another different song of praise is recorded for Solomon. He is a man who knows a more established nation and has built the temple as a place where the glory of the Lord may dwell. As the Ark of the Covenant is brought into the newly built temple, Solomon offers a prayer of praise and dedication

(1 Kgs. 8:15-53, 56-61). The Lord is praised for keeping his covenant of love and the promise to his father David of a dwelling place on earth. Yet he asks that the promise of God's very presence be fulfilled, even though the heavens cannot contain him, and that the Lord hears the prayers of his people. He asks that in the temple the Lord be judge, forgiving the people's sin, hearing their prayers, and the prayers of foreigners, and blessing his people with his continued presence. The account of the same event in 2 Chronicles, with parallel material, gives a good indication of the nature of praise at the dedication of the temple as singers use the refrain: 'He is good; his love endures for ever' (2 Chron. 5:13); and the account records the presence of the Lord in a cloud, such that the priests could not perform their service as the glory of the Lord filled the temple (2 Chron. 5:13; 7:1). Praise shouts are also evident in the book of Ezra as the temple is rebuilt after exile. Again a short refrain is used to the Lord: 'He is good; his love to Israel endures for ever' (Ezra 3:11). This expectation of the presence of God in response to praise is a characteristic feature of charismatic spirituality, and short and repetitive phrases of praise are commonly used.

Some of these themes have been recorded by the New Testament writers as songs of praise. In Luke 1:46-55 we read of Mary's song, known to many of us as the *Magnificat*. This is a beautiful song of praise as Mary reflects on what the Lord is doing in her life. He has chosen her as an instrument of his providence and a person of humility to be exalted as the mother of the Lord Jesus Christ. This is followed later in the same chapter with Zechariah's song (Luke 1:67-79), in which the father of John the Baptist, full of the Holy Spirit, praises the Lord for the salvation about to be revealed and to be prepared by his own son as the forerunner to the Messiah. Staying with Luke's Gospel, we also read of the Song of Simeon (Luke 2:28-32), known as the *Nunc Dimittis*, as he gives thanks for the Saviour of the world. Simeon can now be dismissed in peace because he has seen the salvation prepared by God in the sight of all and as a light to the nations for the glory of his people.

The book of Revelation gives us many pictures of the completion of all things. Some of these pictures are less clear to us because of the nature of the imagery and our distance from the book's original time and place. However, of all the pictures given, it is perhaps the picture of worship that offers us one of the clearest images. In the final book of the canon of Scripture, we have a catalogue of songs of praise. These songs of praise are located around the throne in heaven occupied by the Lord God Almighty and in the centre of the throne the Lamb who was slain (Rev. 4:1–514). Around the throne of God are the twenty-four elders and the four living creatures and many angels, thousands upon ten thousand times ten thousand (5:11). In this context we read of a number of songs of praise as the narrative unfolds. These include:

'Holy, holy, holy
is the Lord God Almighty,
who was, and is, and is to come.'
(*four living creatures*, 4:8)

'You are worthy, our Lord and God,
to receive glory and honour and power,
for you created all things,
and by your will they were created and have their being.'
(*twenty-four elders*, 4:11)

'You are worthy to take the scroll and to open its seals,
because you were slain, and with your blood you
     purchased people for God
from every tribe and language and people and nation.
You have made them to be a kingdom and priests to serve
     our God,
and they will reign on the earth.'
(*four living creatures and twenty-four elders*, 5:9-10)

'Worthy is the Lamb, who was slain,
to receive power and wealth and wisdom and strength

and honour and glory and praise!'
(*living creatures and the elders*, 5:12)

'To him who sits on the throne and to the Lamb
be praise and honour and glory and power
for ever and ever!'
(*every creature*, 5:13)

Subsequently, other songs are sung by the multitudes before the throne (7:10) and by the angels, living creatures and elders (7:12). Loud voices proclaim the consummation of the kingdom of God (11:15) and the elders continue their worship of the God who will judge (11:17-18). Another loud voice both praises God because of the work of the Lamb and the testimony of the saints and exhorts the heavens to praise and the earth to fear because of the presence of the devil (12:10-12). This victory is again used in praise as the song of the Lamb (15:3-4) antici-pates the completion of all things. The angel in charge of the waters praises God for his judgements and there is a response from the altar affirming the true and just judgements of the Lord (16:5-7). As the book of Revelation draws to a close, so the crescendo of praise reaches its climax in chapter 19. In a great roar the multitude shout their praise to God for his salvation and judgements (19:1-3), and the elders and the living creatures cry, 'Amen, Hallelujah!' (19:4). Voices come from the throne inviting the servants of God both great and small who fear him to praise him (19:5), at which point the multitude roar and thunder in shouting: 'Hallelujah! For the Lord God Almighty reigns.' The wedding of the Lamb and the Bride has come and the kingdom is consummated, and blessed are those who have been invited to the wedding feast (19:6-9). These are all themes used by song writers in the charismatic tradition throughout different times and in various places.

With this biblical background as an introduction to the importance of praise and worship within Jewish and early Christian worship and life, I now turn to charismatic spiri-tuality specifically. The aim of this chapter is to give an overview of the general characteristics of charismatic worship and the main features of liturgical style, music and songs will be described. It is through these means that the key dimension of praise in the context of worship can be appreciated within the tradition.

General Characteristics of Contemporary Charismatic Worship

Charismatic spirituality is one that travels. It can be found in the classical Pentecostal denominations like the Assemblies of God and the Black Majority Churches, such as the New Testament Church of Prophecy. But it can also be found in many other denominations such as Anglican, Baptist, Methodist, Presbyterian and Roman Catholic, as well as independent charismatic churches known as the New Church Movement and the later denomination associated with John Wimber, the Vineyard Church. In each of these denominations it will have a slightly different contextualized form because the ways in which the spirituality is embodied will vary enormously as other factors come into play. Therefore, a tradition that emphasises eucharistic worship as central will need to accommodate the distinctive characteristics of charismatic worship around that focus. Similarly, for denominations stressing the significance of the preached word in worship there will need to be some accommodation. However, despite these differences of tradition and liturgical structures, there are common elements that constitute characteristics. I shall focus on that which is distinctive and, for the moment at least, leave aside other features (e.g. Bible reading and the sacraments).

In many settings there is an informal context to charismatic worship. This element is increasingly the case, with clergy discarding liturgical vesture in favour of casual clothes. Of course, in some churches, for example the Black Majority Churches, smart dress remains the norm, but for the average British, and I suspect North American worshipper, jeans and a casual shirt would not be uncommon.

This informality is usually accompanied by an amount of time allocated for social engagement, either through opportunities for conversation at the beginning of a service or through a time for refreshments at the end. This informality provides a significant characteristic because it enables people to engage with others and with God in an informal social context. As such it is a prelude to intimacy in worship, which is so important for charismatic spirituality. In other words, people are prepared to meet with God in worship by means of a social context that is friendly and informal.

The musical style of charismatic worship is very obviously contemporary. Even the older hymns are given a contemporary feel with the addition of different melodies and a drummer's backbeat. Visitors to charismatic churches may be surprised to encounter the sheer energy with which worshippers start their services. It may sound more like a rock concert than a church service. However, it is usually the case that energetic praise songs give way to more reflective songs that draw the worshipper into a quieter mode of singing. It is also true, as with all things contemporary, that favourite songs change much more quickly than with traditional worship. For example, the songs of the 1980s might be sung in some churches but in many cases have been replaced by 1990s' and post-2000 offerings. At the current time there is a new range of songs in use and with time the songs of the 1990s will be used only occasionally.

The experience of singing worship songs in a charismatic setting will look considerably different to traditional worship for a number of reasons. Typically during the first part of a service (in the search phase of the spirituality), the congregation will be expected to sing a number of songs that have been linked together as a kind of medley. The words for the songs will be displayed either through the (now outdated) overhead projector screen or through the screen displaying words projected from a PowerPoint computer presentation. There are usually no books (or they are an option) and the expectation is that people are free to engage in worship with enthusiasm unconstrained by a book in their hands. This means that people are free to use their arms and hands to raise them to heaven. They are also free to clap, dance, jump and sway should they wish to do so in time to the rhythm of the music. Generally people are free to stand or to sit as they sing, but in practice the congregation would tend to do similar things at the same time. Songs are memorised and internalised in a much greater way than a book-holding culture would expect and this is an important feature to understand.

There is full participation for those who have embraced the spirituality. In the singing of hymns there is an energetic engagement with praise. When there are readings from the Bible many participants will follow the text from their own copies that they have brought to church. During the sermon there is often an interactive style of preaching that does not allow the hearer 'to go to sleep' – they may be asked a question and a reply will be expected! In some churches the congregation can interrupt the preacher with shouts of 'Hallelujah' and 'Praise God'. During the praise phase and when there is a pause, or when the leader so designates, there may be opportunity for a contribution from the congregation. These contributions can vary and can include the use of spiritual gifts such as prophecy or speaking in tongues, or indeed the opportunity to give a testimony for the encouragement of those present. Such participation represents the spontaneity that is present within the spirituality to respond to the God who is alive and is present with us now. This leads on to my next point.

Charismatic spirituality is associated with the use of spiritual gifts, perhaps far more than any other aspect of the tradition. The gifts are understood to be capacities and events through which God encounters individuals and worshipping congregations by means of his Spirit. Thus speaking in tongues, whereby seemingly gibberish sounds are spoken loudly or quietly, either by an individual or by individuals in concert, or indeed sung together at a point in the service, is regarded as a symbol of divine-human encounter. Where there is an audible and distinct expression of tongues speech that is interpreted and given meaning, then it is regarded as having parity with prophecy. Prophecy itself is regarded as a Spirit-inspired message directed to the congregation for the purpose of insight and edification, although occasionally containing predictive elements. The effect of such lay participation is to democratise spiritual power, so that it no longer resides in the hands of the leadership but is understood to belong to the whole people of God.

Prayer ministry is an important dimension of charismatic spirituality and in recent years has been given enormous attention. This usually occurs towards the end of the church service when people are invited to come forward and receive prayer for matters that concern them. In some contexts words of knowledge are read out to encourage people to come forward and be prayed for. These words of knowledge can be, for example, medical conditions, or personal circumstances or needs. During the height of the so-called 'Toronto Blessing', it was during the ministry time that certain physical manifestations occurred, such as people falling over, laughing, jumping, crying and making strange noises. These phenomena attracted an enormous amount of attention but in fact they have been happening for some considerable time, and have generally been associated with various forms of revivalism. It is during this particular phase of the spirituality process that the focus of charismatic spirituality is most clearly seen. Very often in dramatic fashion individuals and groups are understood and expected to encounter the Spirit of God.

Prayer more generally is a characteristic that permeates the worship service. In the preparation for worship many members will have spent time in prayer, waiting upon God and asking him to reveal something that they might share with the rest of the congregation. At the beginning of worship the leader will pray for the worship time together in an extemporary fashion. He or she may invite others to pray at certain times, either in an audible way so that others can hear and agree, or as part of a prayer shout as the congregation simultaneously prays out aloud together. On some occasions the congregation will be invited to pray together in groups, perhaps in an intercessory way. This may be in response to something that the preacher has said or in response to a prophetic word that has been received by the congregation. Indeed, as I have already noted, prayer is at the heart of charismatic spirituality but in a social and corporate sense. People would be expected to speak out aloud and to pray as the Spirit inspires them to pray in spontaneous ways.

In all of these characteristics there is the sense that people are worshipping God. It is in the exercise of corporate worship that God is encountered by his Spirit in the midst of his people. The dimension of praise provides the beginning of such an encounter and the worship in a broader sense provides the context for other features of the encounter with the Spirit. In order to understand the use of songs in more depth the remainder of the chapter will consider this particular feature more extensively.

Liturgy and Song

Walter J. Hollenweger views Pentecostal and Charismatic public worship as originating from a genuine oral culture and this affects liturgy and worship significantly. In this tradition the liturgical process is not written down but memorised. That is, the sequence of anticipated events is internalised by the members of the group. In this way there is a combination of an understood format and the opportunity for spontaneity to occur. The liturgy is continually in the making and it is a corporate event requiring participation by all those present. Pentecostal liturgies would contain standard elements but would not be named as such. These include: invocation of the Spirit (epiclesis), kyrie, confession of faith, Gloria, eucharistic canon and benediction. However, the service is not structured by means of a set written text and therefore these elements are not always recognisable. Instead, it is structured by means of choruses, that is, short songs, and these can signal a transition from one section of the liturgy to another.[3]

Hollenweger also observes that the use of choruses will vary from one congregation to another. However, the use of these songs within the local context will be understood by members and participants alike. The genre of the liturgy has been likened to a 'jam' session for jazz musicians.[4] Everyone knows the musical theme but there is room for improvisation and creativity in the playing out of the melody with harmonies and counter melodies. In this way there is a dynamic between the orderliness of the theme on the one hand and the spontaneity of the creative contribution on the other.[5] In the mainstream charismatic churches there has been an integration of the oral dynamic of charismatic spirituality within the set written liturgy. Traditional forms of worship that perhaps existed as inspired and spontaneous prayer and song (e.g. some canticles), but have now become written texts, are used in conjunction with spontaneous elements. The move in some traditions from strict authorised liturgical texts to authorised structures with a range of options has also enabled a greater integration to take place (e.g. the Church of England's recent liturgy *Common Worship*).

James H.S. Steven, in his research on the use of songs within charismatic worship in the Church of England, has suggested that the goal of the ritual process of worship is intimacy with God.[6] This is signalled by a move from the up-tempo songs to the more reflective ballads accompanied by a change to the use of singular personal pronouns.[7] It can also be signalled by facial gesture as smiles give way to closed eyes and intense expressions.[8] Intimacy may also be associated with romantic-sounding lyrics and may draw upon biblical imagery of God as lover of one's soul. During this phase of charismatic worship the affective nature of worship is most clearly in focus with the cognitive value of the song being regarded as secondary.[9] However, to acknowledge these features is not to devalue the nature or authenticity of this kind of worship.

Songs and Hymns

Musically, Pentecostalism in the USA was born among African Americans, having its background in what has been termed 'slave religion'. Aspects of this are still very influential today, illustrating the power of the ballad and the song over against the genre of the hymn. The chorus, by its nature, is 'short and sweet'. It is easily learnt, especially when it is repeated many times. In this way it can become memorised and 'you can take it home'.[10] It can be accompanied by a variety of instruments because the melody is relatively simple. Most Pentecostal meetings in the early days of the movement began with singing regardless of whether there was any musical accompaniment or not.[11] Of course, this music is embedded in particular cultures and customs and there will be a great difference between Pentecostals from the southern states of the USA, influenced by 'rhythm and blues', Vineyard churches in California influenced by the John Wimber style choruses and the New Wine churches in the UK influenced by British contemporary music culture. The early British Pentecostals were influenced significantly by the nineteenth-century Evangelical and Holiness traditions of hymns, as well as the earlier eighteenth-century Wesleyan hymns. These hymns are still very much part of the tradition of classical Pentecostalism and are being rediscovered by contemporary Charismatics.[12] However, there is an ever-flowing stream of new songs and choruses arising from the different theological and cultural contexts and new writers continue to be introduced into the worship music scene. In all of these different choruses there are common theological themes but some very different musical styles.

In British Pentecostalism up to the 1960s the style of hymns and choruses was drawn from Methodism and particularly in the 1930s to 1950s reflected the style of the old time music hall. A change occurred with the impact of the renewal movement and the embrace of the folk ballad.[13] This is evident in the collections *Sounds of Living Water* (1974) and *Fresh Sounds* (1976), edited by Jean Harper and Betty Pulkingam.[14] Since that time the influence of contemporary music has been extremely significant with numerous collections of songbooks, such as *Mission Praise* (1980s and combined edition 1990), *Spring Harvest Praise* (from the 1980s) and songbooks to accompany the annual events of *New Wine* and *Soul Survivor* (from the 1990s).

The significance of the impact of Charismatic Renewal worship styles is summarised by D.L. Alford:

> Music contributions of note relating to the charismatic renewal include: (1) the importance of singing psalms and Scripture songs; (2) the heavy use of music for praise and worship, not only in the sanctuary but also in conferences, festivals, small groups, home churches, and in private; (3) use of musical instruments, both formally and informally; (4) a return to emphasis on spirited congregational singing, featuring praise leaders rather than choirs; (5) use of spontaneous and choreographed dance and pageantry; (6) use of drama, mime, and hand-signing; and (7) emphasis on the prophetic role of the musician.[15]

In order to illustrate the kinds of songs that characterise the most recent period two songs have been selected.

The first comes from the most influential British songwriter of the 1970s and 1980s, and to some extent of the 1990s, Graham Kendrick, who has written numerous worship songs. He was especially influential through the annual Easter conference called *Spring Harvest* and the *March for Jesus* walks of the 1980s and early 1990s. He continues to write songs that are widely sung but has recently been eclipsed by younger writers appealing to a new generation. To illustrate his style of song-writing here is one song, written in the style of a hymn.

(Men) My heart is full of admiration for You,
My Lord, my God and King.
(Women) Your excellence, my inspiration,
Your words of grace have made my spirit sing.

(Men) You love what's right and hate all evil,
Therefore Your God sets You on high,
(Women) And on Your head pours oil of gladness,
While fragrance fills Your royal palaces.

All the glory, honour and pow'r belong to You
Belong to You, Jesus Saviour,
Anointed One I worship You
I worship You.

Your throne, O God, will last for ever,
Justice will be Your royal decree.
In majesty, ride out victorious
For righteousness, truth and humility.

Graham Kendrick © 1991 Make Way Music

This song of praise emphasises the power and majesty of God, while the first person pronoun enables those worshipping to appropriate the sentiments directly to themselves. The voices of men and women used to echo each other is a feature of Kendrick songs. It has been copied by other writers but is less popular now than in the 1980s.

In the USA, with the influence of John Wimber and the Third Wave movement, a whole repertoire of songs was established that represented this strand of the tradition. It could be described as middle-of-the-road contemporary music, again using the first person pronoun and reflecting the moment of encounter with the Spirit that has brought transformation to the person concerned. It is sung as a response to the grace of such an encounter and with gratitude for the mercy of God.

I give you all the honour
And praise that's due your name,

For you are the king of glory,
The creator of all things.

And I worship you,
I give my life to you,
I fall down on my knees.
Yes, I worship you,
I give my life to you,
I fall down on my knees.

As your Spirit moves upon me now
You meet my deepest need,
And I lift my hands up to your throne,
Your mercy I've received.

You have broken chains that bound me,
You have set this captive free,
I will lift my voice to praise your name
Through all eternity.

Carl Tuttle © 1982 Shadow Spring Music

In the late 1980s and especially in the 1990s there was established a network of churches called New Wine. Initially New Wine was simply a family holiday for St Andrew's Church, Chorleywood. This has grown into a network of hundreds of churches and thousands of people in the UK, with its work spreading to other parts of Europe and North America. It is an Anglican version of the Third Wave, but in recent years has come to embrace other denominations including some Baptist and Independent Charismatic churches. Out of this context, a new generation of songwriters have emerged such as Matt Redman, Martin Smith and Tim Hughes.

Charismatic spirituality is a global phenomenon and parallel to this period in the 1990s there emerged in Australia a slightly different style of renewal song from a group known as the Hillsong writers, and especially Darlene Zschech. Often as the songs are published there is an explanation regarding the song and biblical passages are referred to as sources of inspiration for the writer. Many of the songs are very upbeat praise songs and joy is given a high priority.[16] With so many songwriters producing various types of songs, is it possible to create a typology so that we may understand the hymnody better?

Classifying Charismatic Songs: Is There a Typology?

Victoria Cooke has explored the use of charismatic choruses and songs in extended times of singing, often called the 'worship time' as part of a church service.[17] In particular, she considers the theological content of these songs. She asks the question: what makes a song identifiable as being 'charismatic'? In response, she follows the typology developed by Jeremy Begbie around 1991.[18] However, she believes that the most recent renewal songs move beyond Begbie's typology and that a new classification is required. Therefore, her typology includes the following categories and descriptions:

- *songs of praise*: these are typically up-tempo and are addressed directly to God or Jesus Christ;
- *songs of love and commitment*: these are sung directly to the Father or Jesus Christ or God and express the sentiment of love. In addition there are songs of love that include a response of commitment to offer one's life to God;
- *songs of intercession*: these have included, especially in the 1960s and 1970s, songs of spiritual warfare that declared the victory of the kingdom of God over the powers of darkness. Cooke notes that they are less widely used today and that they have been replaced by songs expressing God's ability to change lives and more general intercessory songs;
- *songs of ministry*: these songs fall into two main types. Some songs are written to be sung to a congregation rather than by a congregation and aim to enable people to be open to God. They encourage people to receive prayer for their

needs. Other songs focus on God's nature and attributes, thus drawing the worshipper into a reflective and intimate sense of God's presence;

- *songs of awe and glory*: these songs relate the transcendent God to the worshipping congregation and celebrate the encounter of such transcendence in an immediate way.

The categories created by Cooke are not intended to be definitive but are simply approximate ones giving a general typology that may not cover every song. Indeed, just as Begbie's typology has been redefined by Cooke, so hers may be recast in due course. Nevertheless, this typology is a useful one and adds another dimension to the spirituality process described earlier. If the process of charismatic spirituality is described as search-encounter-transformation, then songs can be used flexibly within that process. Songs of praise may start the process in the search phase and songs of awe and glory and ministry may represent the encounter phase, as well as songs of love and commitment. Songs of intercession may express the transformation phase as change within the individual is expressed and change within the wider society and the world is sought.

Conclusion

This chapter has described worship and praise within contemporary charismatic spirituality, although variations must be expected according to the influence of contexts, cultures and church traditions. Songs associated with charismatic spirituality display a conviction that God himself is the primary agent in worship and that through them he is establishing and sustaining a personal relationship with the worshippers. These songs are accessible to today's societies in ways in which traditional hymnody may not be.[19] Songs of praise are essential to charismatic spirituality and without their use the tradition simply would not be the same. This is because *gratitude* marks the character of those who have encountered the Spirit.

Gratitude for God's love and mercy *leads to praise*. In praise God is honoured and the Spirit is expected to meet with his people once again. As the offer of praise turns to the encounter with the Spirit, so people draw close to God through words of intimacy that enable an 'affective alliance' to be made and sustained.[20] This intimacy is also empowering so that lives are changed and the change of others is sought through prayer and intercession. The narrative of God's salvation continuing through and by means of his people today, together with the symbols and practices used in the ritual of worship, reinforces the value of praise as belonging to the true worship of the triune God by means of his Spirit.

4. INSPIRED SPEECH

Introduction

In charismatic spirituality inspired speech is a constant thread that runs right through its process and is seen at various points in the framework. It is, of course, supremely located at the encounter phase and its significance is understood in relation to transformation. It contains a number of features such as the reception of revelation through 'words', pictures, visions and dreams; the relay of that revelation through prophetic messages, words of wisdom and words of knowledge; as well as the inspiration in prayer, testimony and preaching. This inspiration can come in an intense and, on occasions, in an overwhelming manner, while at other times it is less obvious and may be part and parcel of the routine of life. To claim 'inspiration' is to claim the influence of God in a directly mediated manner, which subsequently, and/or simultaneously, results in some form of speech. The intelligibility of this speech may vary, with the gift of speaking in tongues being an identifying mark of charismatic spirituality, certainly as it has been expressed through Holiness, Pentecostal and later Charismatic movements.

The Scriptures contain very many examples of God communicating with people. Genesis 2:16 is the first direct example of God speaking to a person, in this case Adam, and, whatever the literary genre of Genesis 2, the fact that God communicates with humans is recorded early in the canon sets the scene for ongoing divine revelation and accompanying inspired speech. Again at the other end of the canon, the book of Revelation as a vision to John on the island of Patmos, provides in a different literary genre another example of revelation, this time by means of an intermediary.

In the early few chapters of Genesis, the Lord addresses characters directly, for example Adam and Eve (chs. 2–3), Cain (ch. 4), Noah (chs. 6–9) and Abram (ch. 12). Indeed, once the narrative arrives at the character of Abram/Abraham there is a fairly constant stream of divine revelation in various ways. This is recorded as direct speech (12:1; 22:1), vision (15:1), word and illustration (15:4-5), dream (15:13-16; 20:3), via angels (16:7-11; 22:15), theophany (17:1-22) and via three (apparent?) human visitors (18:1-16). We also have an example of Abraham engaging in a protracted conversation with the Lord regarding the fate of Sodom (18:20-33).

In the remainder of the book of Genesis, we find the Lord appearing to people mostly in dreams and visions. For example, there is Jacob's dream at Bethel (28:10-16), possibly his wrestling with God at the ford of Jabbok (32:22-30) and, in his old age, en route to Egypt (46:1-4). Joseph's dreams are famous (ch. 37); and later in Egypt Joseph becomes the interpreter of other people's dreams with the help of the Lord (chs. 40–1), including Pharaoh's to his own advantage and to that of the people of Israel. However, theophanies make a return once we arrive at Exodus and Moses' encounter with the Lord at the burning bush (Exod. 3:2-22). This episode contains the clearest example yet of a theophany that reveals something of God's nature (the divine name, 3:14) and gives the prophet a message as well. Moses is sent by the Lord to the people of Israel with a clear message of liberation. Further revelation is recorded in the dialogues between the Lord and Moses (with Aaron) throughout the book of Exodus. The culmination of this revelation is situated on Mount Sinai, with the establishment of the covenant and the reception of the Ten Commandments (Exod. 19:1–20:17). In addition, other laws are recorded as revealed and delivered by Moses to the people (Exod. 21:1–23:19). In this way Moses becomes the archetypal prophet: the one who receives divine revelation and passes it on to the people of God. He is described as the one to whom the Lord would speak face to face as with a friend (Exod. 33:11). There is something highly unique about Moses, since he is the mediator of the Old Covenant, and knows unusual intimacy with God, so much so that God calls him his friend (Num. 12:6-8). Revelation through occasions of divine intimacy is a recurrent theme in contemporary charismatic spirituality.

Throughout the books of the Old Testament we read of various prophecies and prophetic strategies whereby God reveals his will and people hear inspired speech. Some of these appear strange to us, such as the oracle spoken via Balaam's donkey (Num. 22:28-31). There are prophetic schools associated with the period of Samuel (1 Sam. 10:5) and Elijah and Elisha (2 Kgs. 2:3), but above all there are recognised and significant prophets through whom divine revelation is delivered to the people of Israel. These include Samuel, Elijah and Elijah, as well as Nathan (2 Sam. 12), Ahijah (1 Kgs. 14), and Micaiah (1 Kgs. 22). Some of the prophets have been so significant that their prophecies have been written down and appear as major prophetic books (Isaiah, Jeremiah and Ezekiel) and as minor prophetic books (Hosea, Joel, Amos, Obadiah, Jonah, Micah, Nahum, Habakkuk, Zephaniah, Haggai, Zechariah and Malachi). Whatever the textual transmission and redaction of these canonical books, we have contained within them illustrations of Old Testament prophecy, delivered within specific contexts over a protracted period of history. The prophecies contain very different content and the delivery of the messages can vary, from straightforward announcement to symbolic action, parables, the interpretations of dreams and the naming of children.

Once we arrive at the New Testament, we discover that despite the vast difference in time from, say, Moses to Jesus, there is clear continuity of prophetic activity. The birth of John the Baptist is foretold by an angel (Luke 1:13-17) and an angel instructs Joseph to take Mary as his wife and to flee to Egypt after the visit of the Magi (Matt. 1:20-1; 2:13). Of course, Jesus Christ is the prophet par excellence, upon whom the Spirit descends and anoints for ministry and through whom the announcement of the reign of God is inaugurated. It is he who announces the day of the Lord and the restoration of Israel (Luke 4:18-19). He is the supreme prophet because he is the very Word of God himself (John 1.1-14). And yet he is the one through whom the Spirit is given in fulfilment of the promises of old (John 20:21-3; Acts 2.33). This prophetic gift is bestowed by the Spirit upon the disciples, thus fulfilling Moses' wish that all God's people would be prophets (Num. 11:29). The Spirit in Jewish thinking at the time was understood to be 'the Spirit of Prophecy' and the means by which divine revelation and inspiration would be extended to the whole people of God for his praise and glory. This expectation is encapsulated in the prophecy of Joel fulfilled on the Day of Pentecost:

> 'In the last days, God says,
> I will pour out my Spirit on all people.
> Your sons and daughters will prophesy,
> your young men will see visions,
> your old men will dream dreams.
> Even on my servants, both men and women,
> I will pour out my Spirit in those days,
> and they will prophesy.'
> (Acts 2:17-18, quoting Joel 2:28-9)

The narrative of Acts displays this expectation as Philip is instructed by an angel (8:26), Saul meets the risen Christ (9:3-6), the Lord appears to Ananias in a vision (9:10-16) as well as to Peter (10:9-16). Paul receives direction from prophets (13:1-2) and from a vision of a Macedonian man (16:9). Such divine leading is regarded as normal within the narrative of Acts. It is also discussed in the first letter of Paul to the Corinthian church, where he lays down instructions for its proper usage in the assembly. It is regarded as an important gift and one that should not be hijacked by powerful individuals but rather used for the edification of the whole group (1 Cor. 14). The gift of speaking in tongues can approximate to prophecy when it is accompanied by an interpretation and this is to be preferred in the congregational setting.

Finally, we come to the Revelation of John. Again an angel is used to guide the prophet in receiving and understanding the revelation. John writes down what he sees and hears so that it is recorded for the Church's use. The readers are blessed if they both read it and take its message to heart (1:3). Along with these blessings at the beginning of the book, there are curses at the end for those who use the book improperly. If anyone adds or takes away from the prophecy, then they are cursed by loosing their share in the tree of life and the holy city, both metaphors for eternal life (22:18-19).

Again, the biblical account forms the background to understanding inspired speech within charismatic spirituality. The aim of this chapter is to outline the understandings of inspired speech within the contemporary charismatic tradition in order to appreciate its significance. I begin by looking more closely at the Day of Pentecost, followed by a consideration of revelatory experiences and the categories used to describe them before closing with reflections on the assessment of inspired speech within the tradition.

The Day of Pentecost: Inspired Speech Renewed

The account of the Day of Pentecost is one of the most significant passages in the whole of Scripture for those identifying with charismatic spirituality because in it we read how the event completes the inauguration of the kingdom of God. In Acts 2:33 we read that Jesus Christ, now risen and exalted, received the Spirit afresh from the Father in order to 'pour' him out on the disciples. This fulfils his earlier promise that the disciples would receive power with the reception of the Spirit to be witnesses to Christ (Acts 1:8). This power to witness is linked to a dramatic reception of God's Spirit, who is also referred to as the 'Spirit of prophecy', although 'prophecy' is construed in a very broad sense. Thus, it provides the basis for inspired speech and action displayed throughout the remainder of the book of Acts, as noted above.

The narrative of Acts chapter 2 describes how the extended company of disciples were 'all together in one place', when the sound like the blowing of a mighty wind filled the house and they saw what seemed like 'tongues of fire' resting on each person's head. This 'filling' of the Holy Spirit resulted in inspired speech as they began to speak in 'other' tongues. These 'other' tongues were heard by a crowd that was bewildered to discover a group of Galileans speaking different dialects. They were amazed to hear the disciples 'declare the wonders of God' in their own languages (Acts 2:11). Clearly inspired praise is heard by means of xenolalia (foreign languages). Most Pentecostal and charismatic commentators on this passage would agree that it is inspired speech rather than inspired hearing. The various declarations of praise were understood in real language terms by the hearers.

Peter interprets this event in relation to Joel 2:28-30 and the Jewish expectation that the 'Spirit of prophecy' would one day return to the people of Israel. It is a Spirit bringing inspired speech in an egalitarian sense: *all* may experience prophecy via words, visions and dreams. And as such it is a sign that the end has begun to arrive, hence the reference to 'apocalyptic' (end-time) language common to that period, and that salvation is now universally available (Acts 2:21). There are echoes of the Sinai theophany and the giving of the law. Indeed the Jews at the time had begun to associate the feast of Pentecost with the giving of the law. The theophanic qualities of the narrative suggest that there is indeed strong continuity with that tradition, and that the giving of revelation through the law had now been fulfilled by the giving of revelation through the 'Spirit of prophecy'. This means of communication with God can therefore be traced throughout the narrative of Acts as individuals and groups respond to certain promptings, messages and encounters with the Spirit.

Encountering the Spirit as the central motif of charismatic spirituality has its basis in an experiential reality. But this reality is given expression by means of biblical categories as understood within the contemporary tradition. Therefore it is impossible to disentangle experience from conceptual categories used to describe and receive such experiences. However, what may be done is to attempt to delineate the kinds of experiences that people have as well as the kinds of concepts used to describe them, whilst acknowledging the nature of this inter-relationship.

Revelatory Experiences

In the literature of the Pentecostal and Charismatic movements there are various examples of people receiving messages from God via words, or a sense of what it is that God is inspiring them to understand and say, or a picture, vision or dream conveyed via internal mental processes. In previous work on the subject of prophecy, I suggested that most prophetic speech in the context of prayer and worship is based upon a prior (although not always) revelatory experience as well as a prompting to speak, hence 'inspired'.[1] I offer a number of examples from popular charismatic writers to illustrate my point.

John Wimber gives the following example from an aeroplane journey:

> Shortly after take-off, I pushed back the reclining seat and re-adjusted the seat belt, preparing to relax. My eyes wandered around the cabin, not looking at anything in particular. Seated across the aisle from me was a middle-aged man: a business man, to judge from his appearance, nothing unusual or noteworthy about him. But in the split second my eyes happened to be cast in his direction I saw something that startled me. Written across his face, in very clear and distinct letters, I thought I saw the word 'adultery'. I blinked, rubbed my eyes, and looked again. It

was still there. 'Adultery'. I was seeing it, not with my natural eyes, but in my mind's eye. No one else on the plane, I am sure, saw it. It was the Spirit of God communicating with me. The fact that it was a spiritual reality made it no less real.[2]

Wimber then discusses how this 'revelation' prompted him, reluctantly, to have a conversation with the person concerned as a means of entering into an evangelistic opportunity. Such a conversation would therefore be inspired in the sense that it was prompted by God and given direction.

At other times the reception of a message that becomes the basis for inspired speech can be less precise. A specific sense of what it is that God is prompting the recipient to 'pass on' is given to the person. They are then in the position of weighing up what it is that God wants them to speak, to whom and in what context. Bruce Yocum gives a useful summary of this idea:

> Many times when we receive prophecy, we will not receive specific words to speak. Instead, we will be given a very clear sense of the message God wants spoken. By a 'sense of the message', I mean more than a general idea of what God wants to say. I mean a clear, even precise, understanding of the specific message the Lord is giving...Many times I feel that the Lord wants to speak, I receive a clear understanding of the message, but do not immediately know how to say it. So I must apply the right words for the message myself. Because I do have a clear sense of the message, I can tell when I have discovered the correct way to express it.[3]

It is interesting to observe that in this account the understanding is of a 'specific' message rather than a 'general' message. However, this needs to be expressed in the words of the person himself or herself. This interpretative process can vary and the outcome can be influenced by the prevailing local culture in terms of the style of language employed.

Joyce Huggett describes how a person known to her received a picture whilst struggling in prayer with God:

> As she continued to pour out the bitterness of her soul to God, she described her life to him as nothing more than fragments of her former self. While she stood, silent and still before God, into her mind came a picture of the fragments she had described: they littered the ground like many pieces of red clay. As she gazed at the broken vessel representing her life, into the picture came Jesus. She saw the tenderness of his face and observed the sensitivity of his fingers as he stooped down and started to turn over those forlorn fragments. 'Suddenly he started to piece them together', she told me. 'He assured me that, though the vessel was a mess, every tiny piece of the pot was precious. I watched the skill with which he put the pieces together again. He re-created that vessel. He showed me that it would be even more beautiful than it had been before and much more useful.' Then he glazed it and held it up for me to see. I couldn't see a single sign of the joins where the cracked parts had been pressed back together.[4]

This account illustrates both the personal nature of prayer and the ways in which visual imagery in the form of mental pictures can constitute the basis of inspired speech. Typically this experience could be described in the context of ministry to others as well as a basis for possible testimony.

Occasionally someone may receive a physical sensation that forms the basis for some type of prophetic speech. For example, Barry Kissell describes how a particular symptom or illness can be received by a member of the congregation temporarily in order to impart knowledge to another encouraging that person to receive prayer ministry. It may be a kind of pain or headache or unusual physical symptom, which is offered as a word of knowledge to the congregation.[5]

At other times a person may simply be inspired to speak out a message in the congregational setting. They do not know the message in advance, but feel so compelled to speak that they trust the message will be given in the process of speaking. This only makes sense, of course, when we realise that in charismatic worship there are 'spaces' for spontaneous utterances, be they readings from Scripture, prayers, testimonies, tongues speech, prophecies and the sharing of revelations. It is essential to the nature of this type of worship that opportunity for spontaneity is marked out within the ritual of the service.

Categories of Inspired Speech

There are a number of categories that are used to describe and define inspired speech within the charismatic tradition.

Speaking in tongues is the form of inspired speech most associated with Pentecostal and charismatic spirituality since the Azusa Street Revival of 1906.[6] In classical Pentecostalism, speaking in tongues, or glossolalia, is most often understood as the definitive sign or evidence that someone has received a post-conversion blessing of empowerment for ministry, known as baptism in the Spirit. Its subsequent use by the same person in the context of prayer and worship is regarded as its second function, namely as a gift of the Spirit enabling communication with God. Most people who speak in tongues regularly can do so at will and without any heightened sense of emotion (what Hollenweger calls 'cool' tongues). However, for first-time speakers there is often both an overwhelming sense of God's presence and an inescapable urge to articulate the speech that is beginning to be formed in their minds (Hollenweger's 'hot' tongues).[7]

The Charismatic movement of the 1970s and 1980s, after initially embracing the Pentecostal theology of tongues in the 1960s, rejected the idea of it being 'evidence' of the second blessing and instead focused on its use as a gift for prayer and worship. It can be used in the context of praise, as people shout out their praise to God and declare his wonders. It can also be sung and be accompanied by music, in which case it has an aesthetic quality similar to other forms of Christian expression such as plain song or chant. It can also be used in prayer as people intercede for others or for themselves. In these respects it can mirror the charismatic spirituality process of search through praise (offering a sense of beauty and awe), encounter in adoration (offering a sense of intimacy and empowerment) and transformation through intercession (edification of one's faith).[8]

When there is a distinctly audible tongues speech, that is, a speech act heard by everyone in the assembly, and therefore has attracted everyone's attention, there may be a subsequent message or 'interpretation' in the common language of the worshippers. This is understood as corresponding to the type of tongues speech reported by Paul in 1 Corinthians. In this scenario there will be the expectation that someone else, if not the speaker, has an 'interpretation' of the meaning to be conveyed through intelligible speech. The message, once articulated, is understood to correspond to prophecy, although there is some debate regarding its direction (that is, whether the prayer is directed to God or is a message from God).

Prophecy is understood as a gift of the Spirit used within the Christian life for the edification of the congregation and/ or the individual concerned. Again it is understood to be a spontaneous speech act inspired by the Spirit that is specific to the occasion on which it is received. The prophetic message is expected to fulfil the Pauline criteria of 1 Corinthians 14:3, namely: edification, encouragement and consolation. The language of the prophecies can, in many places, sound like echoes of the Old Testament canonical prophets, with messages beginning in the first person singular. The use of King James English can give prophetic messages a highly ritualised feel and is in many respects at odds with the culture of charismatic worship, which is extremely contemporary.

Many Charismatics, however, believe that prophecy is a mixture of the human and the divine and as such needs to be discerned and tested for authenticity.[9] The classical biblical categories of foretelling (prediction) and forthtelling (proclamation) are still used to describe the contemporary phenomenon, although generally predictive prophecies are few in number. Usually, contemporary prophecy found within a worship setting will be short messages. Here is an example cited in the magazine *Renewal*, from 1976:

> My children, I want you to look closely at the festal garment in which you would be clothed. I want you to see the dark thread which is inextricably woven into it, for it is the thread of suffering.
>
> It is the suffering of the Father whose Son was slain before the foundation of the world.
>
> It is the suffering of the Son who set his face steadfast to go to Jerusalem, enduring the cross for the joy that was set before him.
>
> It is the suffering of my Spirit who allows himself to be grieved by your wilfulness and disobedience.
>
> It is the suffering of my church which is bruised and persecuted for my sake, yet not defeated.
>
> I want you to take my oil of joy for mourning, my beauty for ashes, my garment of praise for your spirit of heaviness. But you must realise that you cannot know the power of my Son's resurrection without the fellowship of his sufferings.
>
> If you attempt to remove the dark thread you will find your garment falling into holes, and you will be naked and a laughing stock before the eyes of those who have no love for you or for me.[10]

It is interesting to observe here that the prophecy is delivered in the first person singular, and is ascribed to God the Father, although there is a Trinitarian reference to the suffering of God. It is addressed to a Christian gathering and the opening phrase appears somewhat stereotyped: 'My children'. The metaphor of the festal garment picks up a biblical theme and this is used throughout the message. In this prophecy the perspective of God is presented and the exhortation is not to remove the dark thread of suffering running through the garment. The prophecy closes with a warning of humiliation, should the people fail to appreciate the thread of suffering which marks their calling.

The *word of wisdom* and the *word of knowledge* are also categories that are used in relation to the prophetic and arguably are closely related. In terms of what Paul meant by reference to these terms, the tradition is reasonably unsure. However, certain dominant interpretations have been advanced over the years.

The *word of wisdom* was often understood by classical Pentecostals to refer to information revealed concerning the future. Although this understanding would not necessarily be dismissed it is not the current one within the tradition. The most popular appreciation of this category is that it refers to an inspired application of a piece of knowledge or information. It is the wisely spoken application of knowledge, the wisdom of which is based upon some form of inspiration. Other alternatives are that it refers to a disposition that under-stands the broad purposes of God, or that which is based upon the wisdom of God, including an ability to interpret Scripture. However, the relationship between this category and prophecy remains ambiguous. In some cases there would seem to be a significant overlap, especially if it is deemed that the message articulated contained some form of applied wisdom.

The *word of knowledge* has often been regarded as a companion gift to the *word of wisdom,* being a divinely given fragment of information or knowledge. It is thus interpreted as a revelation of information concerning a person, thing or event, but with a purpose. The purpose of this knowledge makes its application very specific. It is not for general usage but for particular individuals at specific times and places. This fact or insight could not have been known with the natural mind, hence it has a supernatural quality. It is often used within the Third Wave charismatic stream as a way of attending to God in the context of prayer ministry or evan-gelism. That is, people listen out for what God might reveal with respect to their circumstances or the person in front of them and for whom they are praying. It is often based upon a chronologically prior revelatory experience, although sometimes it may be spoken aloud without prior revelation. In this case the revelation comes in the act of speaking.

The *discernment of spirits* was understood by classical Pentecostals to refer to insight into the spirit world, especially in relation to the demonic. The gift is associated with insight into the dispositions of people, the origins of sickness and 'supernatural manifestations'. The use of spiritual sight is regarded as important and, again, it has been associated with prayer ministry and spiritual counselling. Douglas McBain, deviating from this dominant Pentecostal position, suggests that the category be understood as the ability to 'separate spiritual manifestations at their point of origins'.[11] Thus the idea of sifting, separating and distinguishing is advanced. He also suggests that the gift is a mixture of the human and the divine and provides a check on all other claims to inspired speech in that it can offer insights into the motives and meanings of an event or situation.[12]

Prayer is central to charismatic spirituality and it is normally expressed in social ways. It does not really refer to the contemplative style, although some people have attempted to integrate the two. Rather it is primarily a social activity in which people speak out and pray in extempore ways. It can be regarded as inspired speech in the context of spontaneous space in the small group or worship assembly. It is a form of prayer which is expressed 'from the heart' as the person feels 'led by the Lord' to pray. In this expression, the person is inspired to pray aloud so that others can hear and join in and add their voices to the 'amen' that is said. This extempore form of prayer is very common within evangelical and charismatic traditions and most people belonging to these traditions are spiritually energised by it. Of course, it appeals to the more extrovert types of people and each church community will develop its own culture of how these 'open' forms of prayer work. But normally they are led by someone who defines the social space and manages the process.

Sermons may also be inspired, not only in their preparation but also in their delivery. Charismatics, unlike some evangelicals, would not equate prophecy with preaching, that is to say, the view that New Testament prophecy has now been replaced by the preaching of the gospel. Charismatics affirm both prophecy and preaching as complementary but different. However, sermons may contain inspired speech that 'cuts to the heart' and reveals something specific to a particular congregation. This may be because the preacher was so inspired in the act of preaching that s/he departed from the script, or because in the preparation s/he received a 'word from the Lord'.[13]

Testimonies are an important component of charismatic spirituality and give expression to the alignment of individual and social story-telling with the Christian story of the gospel.[14] That is why, traditionally, Pentecostals have turned to the narrative of Luke-Acts as the main source for their theology. It enables them to situate their own story, following their own Pentecost, within the biblical narrative. This means that there is a great emphasis upon continuity with the biblical story. Since the Spirit who acted in such dramatic fashion in the Bible is the same Spirit who acts today, life in the Spirit is a journey with God and a 'way' of salvation. Therefore, when individuals tell a story of what God has done in their lives they do so by referencing themselves and their church community to the overarching gospel story. Because God continues to work in the lives of people today there is an emphasis on individuals giving testimony to what this means. Of course, the tradition has a tendency to over-emphasise the supernatural and the power of God; however, this is recognised and is beginning to be addressed in relation to the biblical notion of lament as a legitimate category for testimony.[15] Testimonies that give expression to pain and suffering without immediate resolution are beginning to be heard.

Conclusion

Sometimes it is easy for those who are less familiar with the charismatic tradition to misunderstand how inspired speech works and is understood to work. It is also the case that participants within the spirituality can misunderstand the nature of the reality they describe. Therefore a couple of points can be made by way of conclusion.

The first point to note is that divine inspiration is not something new and can be traced throughout the biblical narrative in various places and has been claimed throughout church history (see chapter 2). Charismatic spirituality does not doubt this but in fact celebrates it. It is not something to be ashamed of or embarrassed about but something in which to rejoice. 'Encountering the Spirit' as the fundamental motif of the spirituality is the basis for such inspiration and without it there would be no Spirit-led speech. Insofar as all the major Christian traditions have claimed inspiration for the Scriptures, aspects of the tradition and their worshipping patterns, they have appealed to this dimension. What is different in today's world is the scepticism that surrounds such claims to 'inspiration' and the power that can be claimed as a result. Charismatic spirituality holds onto the dimension of inspiration while putting in place certain measures to 'control' the use or abuse of power.

The second point to note is that most Pentecostal and Charismatic leaders, following the injunctions of Paul, take seriously the need to discern the nature of inspired speech. It is not self-authenticating and comprises a mixed phenomenon of the human and the divine. That is why a key book on the subject of prophecy interprets Paul to mean that prophecy is a divinely inspired message that is articulated in human words.[16] Both the origin and expression need to be discerned. Indeed, some writers would go further and suggest that the character of the person also needs to be assessed. Here is an example of a set of criteria from within the Anglican charismatic tradition by which prophecy can be judged. By extension all forms of inspired speech, where intelligible, could be assessed in these terms:

1. Is there any conflict with the supreme authority of Scripture?
2. What is the character and track record of the speaker? Is it consistent with what is being said, and does what is prophesied of a predictive nature actually happen?
3. What is the witness of God's Spirit in the spirits of the hearers, especially the leaders?
4. Is the prophecy consonant with the general direction in which the church is being led? Is it possible, however, that precisely through prophecy God is choosing to adjust the helm a little?
5. Are the leaders and congregation always praying for eyes and ears to perceive and know what God is doing; for receptive hearts to hear his prophetic word?
6. Is there a rigid frame of reference for this, or the recognition that God is sovereign and that his Spirit blows where he wills?[17]

It is also important that all forms of inspired speech are therefore relativised and do not give a platform for claims to new revelation, although this has not always been the case within the history of religion or the broader Christian tradition.

Therefore, inspired speech is valued, promoted and managed within different ecclesial traditions and cultures. Each tradition will have implicit and/or explicit criteria and mechanisms for ensuring that it is used to edify the body of Christ in that place. Indeed, that is the key to understanding the usage of contemporary inspired speech: its purpose is to encourage and edify Christian believers in the context of their spiritual lives together and the mission of the Church in the world.

5. THE SANCTIFIED LIFE

Introduction

The history of Christianity, with its Jewish roots, has been concerned in different ways with the concept of purity or holiness. The emphasis on holiness has been seen to a greater or lesser extent at different time periods in the Church. Charismatic spirituality as manifest through the Pentecostal tradition is an inheritor of the Wesleyan and Holiness movements of the nineteenth century. Aspects of this tradition are to be seen in contemporary expressions of Charismatic Christianity, although the manner in which it is worked out will vary according to contexts and other traditions at play. Nevertheless, the ideas of being holy or becoming holy are important to this tradition and they need to be appreciated as part of its contemporary expression.

The concept of holiness is a thread that runs through the Scriptures and it is used in a number of ways. It is often used to designate people and objects as set apart for the purposes of God. It is used of God to refer to the absolute purity of his essence and character. He is utterly righteous and without fault and exists in a state that is transcendent. Thus it refers to the association of God with others: these others (people and things) attain some form of holiness by virtue of their connection with him. The word 'sanctified' means that which is designated or in the process of being designated holy unto the Lord. Thus when we read in Genesis 1:2 that the Spirit of God (Holy Spirit) hovered over the water, some have suggested that the whole of created life is in some sense sacred because it has been set apart for the purposes of God. Of course, the problem of 'the Fall' introduces the notion of sin that changes the situation. The result of this Fall is to introduce alienation between God and humanity. Sin is not just ignorance, although it can be that, it is not just wilful disobedience to the known laws of God, it is also the incapacity to do the right thing and to be in a right state.

The Old Testament records a number of ways in which the Lord deals with the breach that sin has brought. The Ten Commandments set the basic parameters within which covenant loyalty is to be demonstrated (Exod. 20:1-17; Deut. 5:6-21) and life is to be lived in a holy way. The book of Leviticus stipulates in terms of sacrifices that which can be offered to God in order to rectify the breach. The Aaronic priesthood is provided in order to mediate between the people and it is the mechanism used to deal with sin through the sacrificial system (Lev. 8). But in addition to the system enabling the people to continue in a right relationship to God, there are lifestyle-markers mentioned. These include eating only prescribed foods, that is only those foods considered as clean (Lev. 11), instructions regarding menstrual cycles and childbirth (Lev. 12), infectious skin diseases (Lev. 13–14), bodily discharge (Lev. 15), eating of blood (Lev. 17), certain sexual relations (Lev. 18), improper sacrifices (Lev. 22:17-30), cancellation of debt (Deut. 15) and tithes (Deut. 26). Above all, the Day of Atonement is the annual festival during which the nation's sin is dealt with by the High Priest (Lev. 16).

In the New Testament Jesus Christ is the one who is regarded as fulfilling the Old Testament sacrificial system as both High Priest and as sacrificial lamb. He is the one who represents the nation of Israel, as the mediator of a new/renewed covenant, and as the one who reverses the fortune of humanity as the second Adam. It is through his life, ministry, death, resurrection and ascension that sin is dealt with once and for all, and the possibility of living in relation with a holy God once again made a reality. He is the holy one par excellence and therefore the one who can mediate between sinful humanity on the one hand and a holy and righteous God on the other. It is he who has called a people to follow him and be the people of God in the world: to be a royal priesthood and a holy nation belonging to God. Therefore, we see in the New Testament the apostles seeking to make sense of this new situation from within the Judaism of their day.

This is illustrated in Acts of the Apostles with the issue of the 'unclean' Gentile inclusion into the 'clean' and newly reconstituted people of God. In his vision in Acts 10 Peter is instructed to accept the 'unclean' meat (Gentiles), because God accepts people from every nation who 'fear him and do what is right' (v. 35). The Gentile household of Cornelius receives the Holy Spirit while Peter is speaking so that the Jewish believers present are astounded (v. 45). The same Holy Spirit made Jews and Gentiles one in Christ. The inclusion of the Gentiles is endorsed by the Council of Jerusalem (Acts 15), again because of the Gentile reception of the Holy Spirit and because God had 'purified their hearts by faith' (v. 9). In order to enable fellowship to be sustained the only instructions the Gentiles receive is that they should abstain from 'polluted' food (via idolatry), the meat of strangled animals and blood, and from sexual immorality (v. 20).

Paul considers the problem of sin and the need to lead a righteous life in his epistle to the Romans, where he enjoins his readers to lead lives that are holy. God enables believers to be controlled by his Spirit rather than the sinful nature since the presence of the Spirit indeed defines that person as belonging to Christ (Rom. 8:9). This should result in sanctified and sacrificial living that is holy and pleasing to God (Rom. 12:1). Elsewhere Paul reinforces the Jewish understanding of holiness in relation to sexuality, food and idolatry (1 Cor. 5 and 8) and understands sin as a form of contamination (2 Cor. 7:1). Indeed, sexual purity is a common theme in Paul's letters and is often linked to the presence of the Holy Spirit (1 Thess. 4:3-8). In the disputed Pauline epistle to the Ephesians, Paul defines the people of God as a holy temple indwelt by the Holy Spirit (Eph. 2:21-2). These ideas are also echoed by Peter, as the people of God are instructed to be holy because God is essentially holy (1 Pet. 1:16), thereby exercising a ministry as a holy priesthood offering spiritual sacrifices (2:5) and living as a holy nation belonging to God (2:9).

This biblical overview gives something of the background to the discussion of sanctity and holiness found within the charismatic tradition. In this chapter I aim to build upon these biblical aspects of purity and holiness by considering the importance of the Wesleyan and Holiness traditions for Pentecostal and charismatic spirituality. From this background I consider the ways in which Pentecostal and charismatic approaches use purity themes and reformulate them in very different contexts. In particular, I discuss the ways in which Roman Catholic Charismatic Renewal and contemporary British Pentecostalism have interpreted this theme. In conclusion, I consider the relationship between purity and power and the Trinitarian context for holiness.

The Roots of Contemporary Charismatic Holiness

There are a number of strands that feed into the contemporary expression of holiness within charismatic spirituality. These can be identified as belonging to Wesleyanism, the broader Holiness tradition, the Keswick movement and Pentecostalism.

Donald W. Dayton gives a useful summary of Wesley's theology in relation to our theme and it is worth considering what he says. First of all he cites a helpful summary of the process of salvation in the words of Wesley himself:

> Salvation begins with what is usually termed (and very properly) preventing grace including the first wish to please God, the first dawn of light concerning his will, and the first slight transient conviction of having sinned against him. All these imply some tendency toward life; some degree of salvation; the beginning of a deliverance from a blind, unfeeling heart, quite insensitive to God and

the things of God. Salvation is carried on by convincing grace, usually in Scripture termed repentance; which brings a larger measure of knowledge, and a fuller deliverance of the heart of stone. Afterwards, we experience the proper Christian salvation, whereby, 'through grace' we 'are saved by faith', consisting of those two branches, justification and sanctification. By justification we are saved from the guilt of sin, and restored to the favour of God; by sanctification we are saved from the power and root of sin, and restored to the image of God. All experience, as well as Scripture, shows this salvation to be both instantaneous and gradual. It begins in the moment we are justified in the holy, humble, gentle, patient love of God on man. It gradually increases from that moment, as a 'grain of mustard-seed, which, at first, is the least of all seeds,' but afterwards puts forth large branches, and becomes a great tree; till, in another instant, the heart is cleansed from all sin, and filled with pure love for God and man. But even love increases more and more, till we 'grow up in all things unto Him that is our Head'; till we attain 'the measure of the stature of the fullness of Christ'.[1]

Dayton observes that Wesley's understanding goes beyond forensic justification and emphasises a strong doctrine of sanctification. Wesley's doctrine of 'entire sanctification' (the ability not to transgress a known sin voluntarily) can be interpreted as a form of realised eschatology, although the consideration of Wesley's theology on this matter continues to cause problems for interpreters. For our purposes, it is important to note that although sanctification is viewed as a process, there is also a definite 'moment' when sin has been overcome. In this moment 'inbred sin' as the result of Adam's Fall is dealt with by a second blessing, which purifies the believer of inward sin and enables 'perfect love' towards God and neighbour to be received, thus enabling a perfection of motives and desires.[2] Others in the Methodist movement at the time, namely John Fletcher, argued that the second blessing was also a 'baptism in the Holy Spirit' as well as a cleansing experience.[3]

The spread of Methodism to America led by Thomas Webb, Francis Asbury and Richard Wright brought with it the extension of this theology of sanctification. Vinson Synan notes from the account of an observer at the time that the early Methodist revivalist meetings could be extremely emotional events: 'Some would be seized with a trembling, and in a few moments drop on the floor as if they were dead; while others were embracing each other with streaming eyes, and all were lost in wonder, love and praise'.[4] Shouts of joy and cries of grief were indistinguishable from one another and the noise could be heard for miles around. Thus a 'heart' form of religion was given expression in the colony of America and attracted a great many from the lower strata of society. Indeed, some of the early 'camp meetings', as they were called, for example the Cane Ridge camp of 1800, exhibited phenomena often associated with the so-called 'Toronto Blessing'. These include: falling to the ground, screaming, jerking, 'barking like dogs', laughing and dancing.[5] From this time Methodist revivalism and the 'camp meeting' was established in America and its legacy continues with us to this day.

Towards the middle and end of the nineteenth century the Methodists worked with other smaller holiness groups through camp meetings to promote the teaching of holiness and 'The National Holiness Association' was born and published material to promote its 'second blessing' message.[6] Methodist preachers promoted the message both at home and abroad. For a time it was extremely successful, reaching its peak in America in the 1880s. However, the interdenominational character of the National Holiness Association caused problems for those wishing to promote Methodist church polity. Individuals and groups began to break away from Methodism and establish themselves as Holiness 'bands'. Over the course of the last twenty years of the nineteenth century the Methodist churches began to lessen their

commitment to the Holiness movement and independent
Holiness churches were established between 1895 and 1905.

One of the important aspects of the Wesleyan and Holiness
tradition is the use of 'holiness codes' to define their identity.
For example, at one General Assembly of the Holiness
Church, the Church of God (Tennessee), which was to become
Pentecostal in due course, decided that 'Coca Cola, chewing
gum, rings, bracelets, and earbobs were sinful', thus prohibiting members to use such things. Other churches condemned the use of neckties or the attendance at fairs, or
political parties and work unions.[7] As these churches became
Pentecostal churches (post the Azusa Street Revival) the
same kinds of codes were enforced, for example, prohibiting
mixed bathing, going to the cinema or theatre and the use of
face make-up.[8]

In the UK the Keswick Convention, founded in 1875 and
held in the Lake District, modified the Wesleyan view but
nevertheless maintained holiness ideas, referring to 'practical
holiness' and the possibility of the 'counteraction' of sin.[9] This
teaching was based on a reading of Romans 6:1-14 that
Christians are dead to sin and alive to God in Christ, that the
old self has been crucified with Christ and that Christians
are no longer enslaved to sin; therefore they should yield
themselves to God and become instruments of righteousness.
This was interpreted to mean that faith was the means of
holiness: faith to believe that one is dead to sin and alive to
God, relying on Christ through the Holy Spirit to defeat sin
and promote righteousness every moment of the day, and
using the Spirit's power to resist temptation to do evil. Faith
is the key to freedom from sin and living by faith is a form of
Christian 'higher life'. The sinlessness of the heart was
rejected as false, but the sinlessness of acts as conscious
deliverance from known wrongs was promoted.[10] Thus Keswick kept Wesley's notion of sin (voluntary transgression of a
known law) and promoted the Christian life as potentially
full of victory over temptation and moral weakness. As
Packer states: 'Victory over sin, happiness in Jesus, and a life

full of God is, said the teachers, the richest heritage imaginable, and it is promised in the gospel through the Holy Spirit's ministry to all who are Christ's and have learned the secret of living by faith."[11]

The American Pentecostal movement, associated with the Bible school of Charles Parham at Topeka, Kansas in 1901 and with William J. Seymour and the Azusa Street Revival from 1906, has its roots in the Holiness movement of the period. Both of these men were holiness preachers. The emphasis at the meetings was not simply on experience of sanctification, but also on a third experience of grace or empowerment, known as 'baptism in the Spirit', and evidenced by the phenomenon of speaking in tongues. The early Pentecostals believed in a three-stage process (conversion, sanctification, baptism in the Spirit).[12] This was accepted by early Pentecostal groups until 1908, when W.H. Durham reduced the stages to two and abandoned sanctification as a distinct stage by incorporating it within the conversion stage. Other Pentecostal groups began to follow this teaching in due course. However, despite this integration in many denominations, there remains a commitment to the tradition of holiness and this is expressed in a variety of ways.

It has led to a set of expectations regarding obligation and prohibitions. Hollenweger identifies a number of strands within the ethical domain.[13] Many classical Pentecostals teach tithing, the giving of ten per cent of their income to the ministry and mission of the Church. Sunday is observed as a Sabbath as the Lord's Day for worship, rest and recreation. Pacifism is represented within the tradition and military service is refused by many, although this position is not as strongly represented as it once was. Smoking and drinking alcohol are often rejected, and some food that contains blood (cf. Acts 15:28-9). There is a rejection of worldly pleasures, often associated with music, cinema, theatres, certain fashionable clothing and make-up. Celibacy outside of marriage and fidelity within it is commonly taught. Marriage is therefore esteemed between believers and divorce prohibited, except on the ground of adultery. Although some of these ethical boundary markers are being relaxed, Pentecostals would tend to be fairly conservative with regard to many of these matters.

Roman Catholic Renewal and 'Sanctity'

The Roman Catholic Charismatic Renewal at its height in the 1970s produced many important books and articles, especially from the USA. Since that time the impact of the renewal movement in that tradition has appeared to wane. However, a consideration of the material of the time offers different insights into how various ecclesial traditions have expressed the charismatic tradition. One of the earliest accounts of the influence of Pentecostal and charismatic spirituality within Roman Catholicism is by Edward D. O'Connor.[14] In discussing the effects of the baptism in the Spirit he notes that there is no instant sanctity. The baptism in the Spirit may have removed certain bonds and secured psychological healing but for most people life in the Spirit is part of the process of growing in Christ and is gradual. It places them further along the road to sanctity than would have previously been possible but still they have not arrived. There are no cases of 'instant sanctity', even if the charisms are powerful aids towards sanctity. Thus a progressive growing into holiness is envisaged, with powerful jumps forward and support along the way.

Another Roman Catholic writer, Heribert Mühlen, has also reflected on this area in relation to gifts of the Spirit.[15] In addition to prophecy, tongues and healing, he advocates what he calls socio-critical charisms and it is these that have ethical and therefore holiness dimensions, although the language of 'holiness' is missing. Instead the language of 'purification' is used to describe how the Spirit takes abilities and sets them apart to be used for the kingdom of God. Thus Paul uses the gift of administration to make a collection for the poor, so that there is an equilibrium between rich and poor. This has wider implications for the social involvement of

Christians, since it is an expression of charisma, that is, it is graced (2 Cor. 8:1). Charismatics, like Jesus, should be willing to become poor so that others might become rich (2 Cor. 8.9). Therefore, the implications of this are that the social and charismatic experience of God in worship should flow out into social and political commitment.[16] To be inspired by the Spirit will mean action on behalf of others (Jas. 2:15-17). Mühlen gives the following warning to those who do not see the social and ethical implications of life in the Spirit:

> Baptism of the Spirit takes hold of your powers, including your emotions; but if such an experience estranges you from society, if you think that you are now really able to lead a purely private bourgeois life, it would be better if you had never come into contact with the charismatic renewal. Either you strip your faith of its private character for the sake of society or you remain even in regard to God in a private, segregated existence and – in what you call 'experience of God' – you are perhaps enjoying only your own feelings.[17]

René Laurentin observes that the criticism of the movement with regard to its introspection and concentration on devotion at the expense of the struggle for justice through political engagement has often been made.[18] The concept of 'charity' (love) has been focused upon in a narrow sense of individuals and neighbour rather than in relation to the social structures. He asks: is this not a 'mysticism that distracts from action?'[19] He admits that some adherents who have previously been involved in social issues have sometimes withdrawn when they have received charismatic experiences. However, he maintains that the Spirit has subsequently led them into more demanding involvement, especially in relation to the poor and the marginalised. This, he notes, is true on both sides of the Atlantic, with the establishment of communities committed to social action. At the time of writing he suggested that among Christians generally, those who are most involved in movements for justice are more likely to be from within the Charismatic movement. Whilst this may have been true in the Roman Catholicism of the 1970s, I suspect that it is not so true at least in the present day, even if social concern is still associated with the Pentecostal and charismatic expressions of Christianity.[20]

Contemporary British Pentecostalism

William K. Kay, in a questionnaire survey of contemporary Pentecostal ministers in Britain, considers a number of ethical areas as indicative of how the Holiness tradition continues to be influential.[21] He looks at divorce and remarriage, homosexuality and the holiness code governing leisure activities. Kay's results show that the majority believe that divorce should not bar a minister from continuing his ministry provided that he is the 'innocent' party. The majority of the sample would also disagree with the possibility that a minister who is divorced and remarried should be able to continue in ministry (60%). The prohibition is even higher for a minister who had committed adultery (82.5%). A minister who is a practising homosexual is considered as disqualified for ministry (95.9%). The holiness code was also measured in terms of Christians being able to smoke, gamble, attend the cinema, take part in social dancing, drink alcohol, buy or sell on a Sunday, engage in sport on a Sunday or watch TV on a Sunday. Within the sample the majority agree that Christians should not smoke (91.4%) or gamble (94.0%). Cinema-going is more acceptable than social dancing or drinking alcohol, although some Pentecostal denominations are stricter (Apostolic Church and Church of God) than others (Assemblies of God and Elim). The same pattern can be seen with respect to Sunday leisure activities with the Apostolic Church and Church of God being more rigorous and the Assemblies of God and Elim being less rigorous. This suggests a shift in the Holiness tradition, with the Assemblies of God and Elim accommodating themselves more to the social norms of UK society.

In this regard, Elim, and to some extent the Assemblies of God, are more similar to Charismatics in other non-classical Pentecostal denominations. Charismatic Christians have not had the same sense of indebtedness to the Wesleyan and Holiness traditions as classical Pentecostals.[22] Certainly the New Churches (formerly the House churches) would be conservative in matters of ethics, but would not necessarily construct a holiness code to inform new converts. Rather, certain expressions of holiness as a part of lifestyle would be advanced within the ethos of the community. Therefore, holiness as a process of growing more like Christ, as distinct from one dramatic event, would be advocated. But there is also a reaction against the perceived 'legalism' of earlier generations of Christians, believing that the life in the Spirit brings liberation.[23]

In many ways the contemporary expression of holiness within charismatic spirituality resembles the tensions within Evangelicalism and other traditions concerning how life should be lived in today's world. Instead of a holiness code that functions to set clear social boundaries between those on the inside and those on the outside of the Church, there are now some ambiguities. For example, codes referring to dress, leisure, alcohol and smoking are no longer seen as fundamental to charismatic identity. Indeed, the expression of charismatic spirituality within Roman Catholicism, with very different local cultural forms of expression, has certainly given rise to some conflict between Charismatics of different types. Nevertheless, there are some key concepts that demand attention and enable an understanding of how holiness functions in relation to this form of spirituality. I mention two briefly.

First, there is a clear recognition of the significance of sin in the spiritual life. Sin would tend to be defined in relation to biblical norms and the understanding would be that contravention of biblical norms would require repentance and the reception of forgiveness for the power of the Spirit to be restored in full. Of course, the famous episodes of American

Tele-evangelists confessing their sins of adultery and embezzlement in front of thousands, if not millions, of viewers have done nothing to support the integrity of this aspect in the minds of many, even within the charismatic tradition.

Second, although charismatic spirituality does not necessarily make purity a prerequisite for the reception of power, as many Pentecostals would do, especially in the Holiness Pentecostal traditions, there is an inevitable relation between the two. It is believed that for the dynamism of the Spirit to be continued in the person's life, there must be an ongoing 'infilling' of the Spirit, and the Spirit would by his nature as holy bring to mind those things which require cleansing and restoration. Of course, contemporary Christians are subject to modern ethical debates concerning sexual ethics, sanctity of life issues and global warming as any other Christian would be. How these issues are dealt with will also reflect other theological commitments, as well as the concern to live holy and empowered lives before God and one's neighbour.

Conclusion

I conclude this chapter by reflecting briefly on two theologians, one Pentecostal and the other Charismatic. Simon Chan relates the concept of power to purity in the context of attempting to integrate contemporary Pentecostal theology within the broader tradition of spiritual theology,[24] while Robin Parry aims to situate the charismatic life of holiness within a Trinitarian context.[25] Both are important contributions to the discussion for contemporary theology and spirituality.

In the context of discussing the relationship between Spirit-baptism and spirituality Chan suggests that biblically the charisms (power) are linked to holiness. In other words, charismatic power and its manifestations are linked to an ethical community in a covenant with God. This means that the charismatic life is authenticated by holiness and not by spiritual power (Matt. 7:21-3). Indeed, signs and wonders must normally be understood as flowing from the life of holiness, even if sometimes this may not be the case.[26] For Chan the goal is not to be fixated with the spectacular but to see a 'conjunction of miracles and sanctity'.[27] This conjunction is possible through the virtue of humility, following the example of Christ who is believed by the Holiness-Pentecostal tradition to be the Sanctifier, as well as the Saviour, Baptiser, Healer and Coming King. Chan believes that Christ as Sanctifier needs to be restored to the Pentecostal-charismatic tradition, even if the second Wesleyan stage of 'entire sanctification' cannot now be retrieved. Such a recovery would enable a reintegration of holiness and power within the Christian tradition in ways that would echo the Thomist tradition of miracles being correlated with sainthood. How this might be worked out with regard to other expressions of charismatic Christianity, such as the Third Wave, remains to be seen.

Robin Parry situates Christian ethics within a Trinitarian context as a participation 'in the Son's holy obedience to the Father with the help of the Spirit'.[28] The Father desires our holiness, and it is Christ who breaks the power of sin and makes holiness possible (picking up the theme of Romans 6). The Spirit applies the power of the cross to Christians in order to make them holy. He concludes his discussion with an echo of Irenaeus' metaphor for the Trinity as 'two hands of the Father'. It is a summary that is worth quoting in full:

> [E]thical living is not about pulling ourselves up by our own moral bootstraps. Rather, it all begins with the Father, who longs to reshape our warped humanity so that we can be holy. To that end he reaches out to us with his two hands. The Son took our humanity upon himself and lived in perfect obedience yet absorbed the consequences of our damaged human nature on the cross. At Calvary he mysteriously breaks the power of sin and death over humanity so that those who are 'in him' do not have to be enslaved to sin any longer. The Spirit then

works within the community of believers to reform their actual lives so that the fruits of Christ's work at Calvary work out in practice. As Gordon Fee puts it, 'the coming of the Spirit means not that divine perfection has set in, but "divine infection"'. The place of the believer is to co-operate with God in this work – to walk in the Spirit and resist temptations that come our way, to confess our sins and await patiently the completion of our ethical transformation when the Lord returns.[29]

6. EMPOWERED KINGDOM WITNESS

Introduction

Charismatic spirituality has often been associated with forms of apocalypticism: end-time expectations about the consummation of the kingdom of God. To some extent this is still prevalent but cannot be said to permeate every expression of the tradition. Nevertheless, the kingdom of God is a key theological feature that draws together other themes and enables a coherent picture to be presented of life imbued with this form of spirituality. Indeed, the framework of the kingdom of God has been made popular in recent charismatic understanding since the 1980s because of the influence of John Wimber. Wimber in turn borrowed from the work of New Testament theologian George Eldon Ladd. However, the concept of kingship has a long history in Christianity, not least within classical Pentecostalism as well. The classical Pentecostal traditions have defined a five-fold gospel paradigm, identifying Jesus as Saviour, Baptiser, Healer, Sanctifier and coming King. The emphasis is on the king's return to claim his kingdom in full. Biblical material concerned with the nature of the kingship inaugurated by Jesus is central to the discussion, but it has antecedents within the Old Testament, and the Gospel writers draw upon this material freely.

Throughout the Bible the motifs of king and kingdom are deeply embedded in the different literature. Almost from the earliest of books there is a sense that the people of Israel are special and that God's very presence goes with them (Exod. 33:14). They are unlike the other nations, who rely on human

kings: they have their God as king. So that when the people
wish to designate a king, like Gideon (Judg. 8:22), or ask for
a king (1 Sam. 8), the answer is that the Lord is their king.
However, eventually the Lord relents and a king is appoin-
ted, first Saul, then David and then Solomon. David's reign is
the one that establishes the kingdom and gives Israel its
deepest understanding of what it means to have a king.
Indeed, from his reign come the ideas of a perfect king and a
perfect reign of justice and peace. Nevertheless, there is
retained the idea that God is also Israel's king — perhaps
Israel's only true king and all human versions simply mirror
God's kingship.

In the prophetic literature there is an anticipation of that
day when God will establish his reign of justice and peace. It
will be a kingdom of righteousness (Isa. 32) when Israel will
be restored (Isa. 49:8; David's fallen tent, Amos 9:11) and be
blessed (Joel 3:17); everlasting salvation will be established
(Isa. 52) and the glory of Zion be revealed (Isa. 54; 60). It will
be a great day of judgement and mercy when the Lord will
display his purposes for his people (Zeph. 1:14; Zech. 14; Mal.
3:2; 4:1). Perhaps the most important Old Testament text is
one that is used by Jesus to claim messiahship and to
announce the inauguration of the kingdom of God in the
midst of his people. It is the year of the Lord's favour
announced by Isaiah:

> The Spirit of the Sovereign Lord is on me,
> because the Lord has anointed me to preach good news
>   to the poor.
> He has sent me to bind up the broken-hearted,
> to proclaim freedom for the captives
> and release from darkness for the prisoners,
> to proclaim the year of the Lord's favour
> and the day of vengeance of our God. (Isa. 61:1-2)

This text, announced by Jesus as recorded in Luke 4:18-19,
links the coming of the king and the year of jubilee with his
anointing for the inauguration of the kingdom. It provides the

theological framework for understanding his ministry in the Gospels and indeed the early Church as recorded in the rest of the New Testament.

The anointing of Jesus is a key to the Synoptic Gospels' representation of who Jesus is, and especially for Luke. So Mary conceives a son by the workings of the Holy Spirit (Luke 1:35), witnessed and glorified in the inspired speech of others (Luke 1:41-2). Jesus is anointed with the Spirit again at his baptism (Luke 3:21-2) and subsequently claims his mandate to establish the reign of God (Luke 4:18-19). This is demonstrated throughout the narrative of the Gospels through exorcisms (Luke 4:31-7, 41; 8:26-39; 9:37-43; 11:14-26), including the important interpretation: 'if I drive out demons by the finger of God, then the kingdom of God has come to you' (Luke 11:20); healings (4:38-40; 5:12-14, 17-26; 6:6-9; 7:1-10; 8:43-8; 13:10-13; 18:35-43); raising the dead (Luke 7:11-15; 8:40-56); the restoration of the twelve tribes of Israel (Luke 5:1-11; 6:12-16; 9:1-6); table fellowship with outcasts (Luke 5:27-32; 19:1-10); forgiveness of sinners (Luke 7:36-50); answered prayer (Luke 18:1-8); power over the forces of nature (Luke 8:22-5); the feeding of people (9:10-17); displayed in prefigured glory (9:29-36); enacted symbolically in a reconstituted passover meal (Luke 22:7-38) and the triumphal entry as the people shouted, 'Blessed is the king who comes in the name of the Lord'(Luke 19:28-38); and, of course, the defeat of death itself in resurrection (11:29-32; 24:1-49) and the exaltation as Lord and Christ (Luke 24:50-3; Acts 1:1-11).

Jesus as healer is a constant thread running through the Pentecostal and charismatic traditions, but Charismatics would broaden this category to include 'signs and wonders' more generally. Thus they would appeal to the Gospel records more generally. Here, the birth of Christ by means of the Spirit of God is regarded as a sign of witness to the purposes of God (Matt. 1:18). Other signs follow and they are interpreted by a heavenly voice, for example his baptism and transfiguration (Mark 1:9-11; 9:2-8). Jesus performed many signs and wonders in his ministry signalling his power to save people from disease and sickness. A distinction is made in the Gospels between healing and the exorcism of demons done by Jesus. He also raises the dead (Matt. 9:18-26), walks on water (Matt: 14:25), feeds the 5000 (Matt. 14:13-21) and yet will not bow to the pressure to perform signs for the sake of the signs themselves and celebrity status (Matt. 16:1). Ultimately the greatest sign indicating the validation of his life and ministry is indeed the resurrection: the great reversal when death, the ultimate enemy, is defeated and robbed of its power (Matt. 28). Indeed the ministry of Jesus is bound up with signs and wonders as the power of God's chosen one is displayed for all who would see to see.

The ministry of empowered witness through signs and wonders continues to be seen in the Acts of the Apostles (5:12). These include healing (3:1-9; 8:7; 28:8-9), words of judgement resulting in death (5:1-11), exorcisms (8:7), escape from prison (12:3-19) and no ill effects from a snake bite (28:5-6). In a similar vein to the Acts, Paul is able to summarise his ministry in terms of glorying in his service to God through Christ Jesus and testifying to what Christ has accomplished through him 'by the power of signs and miracles, through the power of the Spirit' (Rom. 15:19). Again, for Paul, the greatest sign is the resurrection of Christ (1 Cor. 15), representing the first fruit of the harvest that is yet to come. Finally, the ministry of healing is described by James in his epistle. He specifies that those who are ill should call upon the elders of the Church to come and anoint the sick with oil and to pray for their healing in faith (Jas. 5:14-15).

Given the background of this biblical material, the aim of this chapter is to outline the nature of this theological theme and to locate within it the key features of empowered witness and signs and wonders. The eschatological tension of the 'now and not yet' of the kingdom is explained as a means of appreciating the limitations in contemporary experience, together with the apocalyptic vision that inspires its adherents.

Empowered Witness: Signs and Wonders

Charismatic spirituality believes that the Church is also anointed by the Spirit to continue the ministry of Jesus until he returns at the end of time. In particular, the anointing upon the Church bestows power, power to witness to the kingdom of God here and now. This power comes via the same anointing that Jesus displayed in signs and wonders. God's reign in the ministry of Jesus is witnessed by means of both a proclamation of the arrival of the kingdom and by a demonstration of its arrival through signs. These signs have been evident throughout the biblical canon and often associated with key moments, but now they are more widely available to the people of God throughout history. Thus Charismatics would trace the signs that are described by Luke in Acts to earlier manifestations in the Old Testament (e.g. Exod. 7; Josh. 10; Judg. 6; 1 Kgs. 17; 2 Kgs. 2, 4, 5).

The New Testament material is interpreted as providing examples and a rationale for expecting similar experiences through the ministry of the Church today. David Pytches, for example, begins his book in the Third Wave strand of tradition with a chapter on signs and wonders.[1] He maintains that the great commission of Matthew 28:18-20 includes the imperative: 'obey everything I have commanded you', and that the 'everything' referred to here includes a ministry of signs and wonders. In the Gospels the disciples participate in the healing ministry of Jesus and this is a model for the Church as evidenced in Acts and should be throughout history. Harvey Cox, in his celebrated book on Pentecostalism, calls this feature *primal piety*, the integration of the mystical experiences of healing, dancing and laughing in the Spirit.[2] This feature of charismatic spirituality breaks the barrier erected between the cognitive and the emotional sides of life, between rationality and symbol or sign, uniting individuals and communities in ways that are holistic.[3] The early Pentecostals of Azusa Street broke down a key racial barrier between Black and White as both embraced the signs of the kingdom and thus became one in witnessing to the unity that is available in Christ.

It is certainly true that the theme of 'signs and wonders' as a feature of empowered kingdom witness has become more at home in non-Western rather than Western societies. Charismatic writers since John Wimber have certainly made much of this phenomenon. They argue that in societies privileging scientific rationalist thinking the 'spirit world' has been submerged or eradicated. Therefore the piety associated with 'primal' societies, to use Cox's category, becomes suspicious. Other naturalistic explanations must be found to account for these apparently strange phenomena. However, in non-Western societies where the worldview entertains the possibility of the spirit-world being much more obviously expressed within the public domain, this spirituality flourishes.[4] The challenge for the charismatic tradition is to show how it can be integrated within Western contexts as well as non-Western ones, where the worldview is less accommodating. Hollenweger suggests that one way this might be accomplished is by beginning with a theology of creation, which is also alive with the Spirit of God, and by integrating natural and supernatural categories.[5]

Eschatological Tension

The kingdom of God is the theological framework for understanding the other features of charismatic spirituality. Most importantly it is the anointing experienced by the king, Jesus Christ, being bestowed upon the Church and continued through history. The kingdom has been inaugurated through the life, ministry, death, resurrection and ascension of the king and will one day be consummated upon his return. In the meantime the Church lives between the times and knows the comfort and power of the Spirit to be with her on the journey until the End of all things. However, evil and suffering continue to mark the world in which we live including the Church.[6]

This tension between the inaugurated reign of God, bringing the 'first fruits' of the harvest, and the consummation of the reign, when the harvest will be fully gathered in, marks the nature of the Christian life. Charismatic spirituality appreciates this tension, although at times the 'now' is stressed at the expense of the 'not yet'. Nevertheless, there is now sufficient understanding of this tension within the tradition to see it as a significant feature. This means that while Charismatic Christians pray for God to demonstrate his power through the life of his Church, there is also the recognition that not all one's prayers are answered and that pain and suffering persist in this world. The inauguration of the kingdom did not result in the manifestation of humanity with resurrection bodies!

In the tradition, this is complicated by the role of faith in the prayer for healing. Following the Gospel tradition there is an emphasis on praying for people to be healed in faith and some exponents of the healing ministry have advocated a strong position on this subject. However, others have stressed the sovereignty of God and the tension of the 'not yet' of the kingdom as reasons why some people are not healed, even if others are healed. It is important to recognise that there are a number of different positions in this area, even if there is a positive regard for the role of faith in life in the kingdom.[7]

This tension is also complicated by the dualism that we find in the New Testament regarding the battle between Christ and Satan in the Gospels. The inauguration and establishment of the kingdom of God through the life, ministry, death and resurrection of Christ means that the powers of darkness are defeated, if not destroyed. The destruction of these powers of darkness will be when the kingdom is consummated and Christ is 'all in all'. In the meantime there is also a dimension of spiritual warfare that characterises the Christian life. Charismatic spirituality, along with many other forms of Christian spirituality, has made much of this. Indeed the dualism between God and Satan can, at times, become too exaggerated, with the third category of the 'natural' or creation being omitted in some Pentecostal and charismatic theologies.[8] Nevertheless, this dimension remains part of the spiritual tradition and gives meaning to prayer and mission.

Empowerment for Witness: Baptism in the Spirit

The empowerment for witness has often been associated within Pentecostalism as belonging to an event called 'baptism in the Spirit'.[9] This denotes a post-conversion occasion when someone is overwhelmed by the presence of the Holy Spirit and evidences that empowerment by speaking in tongues, or by some other sign such as prophecy or dance. In classical Pentecostalism, this event was both subsequent to one's conversion and associated with distinct empowering for mission. It was not that the Holy Spirit had not been received at all, for how can anyone confess that Jesus is Lord or know Jesus as Saviour except by the Spirit? But the promise of empowerment by Jesus to the disciples was subsequent to their Pentecost experience of receiving the Spirit (Acts 1:8; 2:1-4).

This norm is read throughout the rest of the book of Acts. Thus in 10:46 we read that, at the house of Cornelius, as Peter is speaking the Spirit comes upon the hearers and they speak in tongues and praise God. Similarly, in 19:6 Paul places his hands on the disciples of John the Baptist at Ephesus and the Spirit comes upon them and they speak in tongues and prophesy. These are the clearest accounts of speaking in tongues being associated with a dramatic encounter with the Spirit, often interpreted as precedent for the doctrine of baptism in the Spirit. Pentecostals also refer to Acts 8:17 as being of central importance, although it is not explicit with regard to tongues speech. Nevertheless, this passage describes the reception of the Spirit by the Samaritans in a dramatic fashion as a possible subsequent occasion of empowerment.

Early exponents of the Pentecostal experience of baptism in the Spirit and speaking in tongues, such as Michael Harper in the UK, came very close to accepting Pentecostal theology at this point.[10] However, it never became officially established within the Charismatic Renewal and other doctrinal traditions, such as those within Anglicanism and Roman Catholicism, would never have accepted it as such. However, traditional sacramental theology could be reinterpreted to lend support to the ideal that baptism in the Spirit was part of the conversion-initiation process.[11] Subsequent experiences could be an 'actualisation' of an earlier sacramental reception. Therefore the practice of a dramatic experience called baptism in the Spirit was retained, as was the practice of tongues speech, but the idea that tongues speech was the 'sign' of empowerment was never fully established in the Renewalist strand of the tradition. With the advent of the Third Wave movement in the 1980s, the emphasis was not so much upon a second post-conversion experience as the gateway to empowerment and the gifts of the Spirit, but multiple encounters with the Spirit as ongoing empowerment in the Christian life. Ministry in the power of the Spirit and in particular the use of words of knowledge as guidance for evangelism and healing became the focus.

Witness: Mission and Evangelism

The Pentecostal and charismatic traditions would regard witnessing to the presence of Christ by his Spirit in the world as one of the most significant aspects of the Christian life. There are indeed 'souls' to be won for the king and his kingdom. This aspect has become more dominant in some strands than others and can be especially associated with Evangelicalism.[12]

In recent years, two dominant evangelism paradigms have emerged from within the charismatic tradition. The first again comes from the influence of John Wimber and his teaching on *power evangelism*.[13] By this is meant the alignment of spiritual gifts, in particular the word of knowledge/wisdom and the gift of discernment, enabling insight into the person's situation to be gained. Via such gifts of revelation one is able to use the information in a way that opens up the possibility of individuals appreciating their need for God and his interest in them directly. The second approach has also been influenced by Wimber and is associated with process evangelism. It is the Alpha Course developed and marketed by Holy Trinity Church, Brompton, London.[14] This approach is extremely popular and has been used widely in a variety of different contexts. It is based on teaching material on the Christian faith, of an evangelical variety, together with fellowship over a meal and a 'weekend away' when the work of the Holy Spirit is explained and opportunity to experience the person of the Spirit is given. There have been a number of criticisms of this approach to evangelism, and some of these criticisms have a certain degree of force. However, it represents the move away from big evangelistic events to locally run opportunities for engaging with the Christian faith. The distinctive charismatic feature is the emphasis on the Holy Spirit and this is regarded as integral to the course. Therefore it reflects aspects of contemporary charismatic spirituality, aligned to evangelical Anglicanism.

The expressions of charismatic spirituality within contemporary Christianity have been less obviously engaged in social action and community development compared with Roman Catholic Renewalists of the 1970s. However, there are exceptions to this norm and there are examples of what might be called a third approach, which have established social programmes. There is, for example, an independent charismatic church in Liverpool that has pioneered open youth work on a massive scale, with ministry to the homeless and vulnerable people in the city. Increasingly there is recognition that the gospel is holistic and that spirituality connects to the whole of life and therefore should be expressed socially in concrete and practical ways. In this context the mission of the church is set within what might be called 'cosmic dualism', or spiritual warfare. That is, the kingdom of God is in battle with the kingdom of Satan. The

Church understands herself to be in the midst of such a battle as the territory of the city is being won back for God.[15] As a key tool in the armoury, speaking in tongues is used as a means of personal and corporate prayer and empowerment, enabling committed self-sacrificial service to the community for the sake of the gospel.[16] Thus there is a correlation between the use of speaking in tongues within this particular dualistic worldview and social action. This view is supported by the work of Margaret M. Poloma, who carried out a study of a church called 'Blood N Fire' in Atlanta, USA. She confirms these similarities in her account.[17] Whilst there may be some problems with this accentuated dualism, it does form part of the current expression of mission theology in Pentecostal and Charismatic Christianity.

Andrew Lord has written a significant book that seeks to articulate a charismatic theology of mission for today.[18] He suggests that it is based on a set of movements of the Spirit (one might even used the word 'encounters'). The movements are between the particular (individuals and church communities) on the one hand and the universal (others and creation) on the other. The character of the Spirit's movement between the particular and the universal is characterised by the metaphors of 'blessing' (the wonders of God, love, praise and joy, power and witness) and 'yearning' (groans of the 'not yet' of the kingdom, sighs of sorrow, weariness, despair and hopelessness). Therefore he characterises a charismatic understanding of mission as holistic, experiential, contextual, based in community, and offering a distinct spirituality. It is this dynamic vision for mission that can be integrated within other traditions enabling Spirit-shaped mission to be understood. It also adds theological breadth and balance to mission theology in the field.

'Doing the Stuff': Prayer Ministry

Prayer ministry has moved through a variety of different expressions over the course of the last few years. It has its roots in the early Pentecostal tradition of responding to the 'altar' call and the invitation to move to the front of the church for prayer for the baptism in the Spirit. Prayer for healing was added to this practice. The Charismatic movement of the 1970s inherited both these features, but in many churches it was the priest, pastors or elders who prayed for others (I remember doing this as a guest preacher at a Roman Catholic Charismatic Renewal meeting in the late 1980s!). With the advent of John Wimber and his influence in the 1980s the healing ministry has taken a different turn and it is now simply called 'prayer ministry', or as Wimber referred to it as 'doing the stuff'. According to the Wimber model, we pray for the kingdom to come by inviting the Holy Spirit to move upon the person or people. We watch to see if there are any obvious physical responses to that prayer and we 'bless' what God is doing by asking the Lord to do more in the person's life. We are also open to the Spirit's promptings as we pray, offering a word of knowledge into a given prayer situation. This may have the effect of enabling the person to receive ministry from God in a greater and deeper way. After some form of training, many people are involved in praying for others and are thus able to participate in 'every member ministry', which is an important feature of charismatic church life.

Prayer ministry normally occurs either towards the end of the service or occasionally can be the central ritual of the worship. It can be described as a form of Christian ministry that aims to bring the kingdom of God into the lives of people.[19] It is concerned with the whole person: physical, mental, spiritual and social. It takes the eschatological tension seriously and therefore understands both success and failure in seeing people healed and made whole. However, within charismatic spirituality it is something that has moved to the centre of the corporate aspect of worship, along with praise and preaching. A key activity within worship is for people to invite the Holy Spirit to come and encounter others for the sake of the purposes of God. It probably now functions as a distinctive mark of charismatic spirituality, alongside praise and worship and the gifts of the Spirit.

The End: The Apocalyptic Vision

As noted at the beginning of the chapter, the early Pentecostals embraced a five-fold gospel: Jesus as Saviour, Sanctifier, Baptiser, Healer and coming King. For many Pentecostals this pattern was reduced to a four-fold one as the 'foursquare' gospel took precedence, and the emphasis on sanctification was dropped.[20] However, the coming kingship of Jesus is maintained universally within Pentecostalism and has significance for the broader charismatic tradition as well.

In the early years, Pentecostalism often referred to itself as the 'Latter Rain Movement'. This was based on the idea that in Palestine rainfall comes at two main times in the year: in the spring and in the autumn. Thus it accompanies planting and harvesting.[21] Pentecostals understand the first Pentecost to be the early rain accompanying the planting of the Church, while the latter rain *restores* the gifts to the Church in the last days, especially speaking in tongues as the gift of Pentecost, and prepares for the imminent harvest and the return of Christ the king. This expectation gave Pentecostalism a key role in the preparation of the 'Bride' to meet her Lord.[22] Thus the Pentecostal movement linked itself consciously to the narrative of Acts 2 and the apostolic Church, giving it a restoration orientation.[23] In this way, baptism in the Spirit as an empowerment for Christian witness is associated with an expectation of a 'harvest of souls' indicating the imminence of the End.

This expectation that 'Jesus is coming soon' was and still is a key motif in Pentecostalism and to some extent it has been transferred to the Charismatic movement and forms part of charismatic spirituality. The link of the coming of Christ with the coming of the Spirit is something that can be found in the early Church, especially Acts 2 and the Joel prophecy. Pentecostal theology has generally been premillennialist: that is, the belief that the return of Christ will inaugurate a millennial kingdom on earth. Certain sectors of the British House Church Movement of the 1970s also embraced this view,[24] but many Charismatics in other denominational traditions have not done so. For example, many Evangelicals in the UK are amillennialist and thus, while praying for the return of Christ, do not associate it with a millennial kingdom on earth. This is in contrast to Methodist, Holiness and revivalist traditions of the nineteenth century, which were postmillennialist, expecting the millennium period to precede the return of Christ, thus making his return less imminent.[25] With the social upheavals of the later nineteenth and early twentieth centuries, the belief that the world would improve and thus be ready for Christ's return began to collapse. Today the dominant Pentecostal vision is premillennialist while the broader Charismatic movement can be classified as amillennialist, or simply content to state that Christ will return at some unknown future date in history and leave it at that.

Conclusion

Empowered kingdom witness is a major theme in charismatic spirituality and without its recognition the tradition cannot be properly understood. The category of the kingdom of God is central to this theme, as is the idea that Christians are full participants in it thereby witnessing to God's reign for the glory of the king. This category allows charismatic spirituality to draw its participants into an activist form of spirituality because there is work to be done and blessings to be enjoyed and shared with others. We are to engage in working and witnessing for the king as the highest vocation and calling. To be sure, there are moments of passivity when we receive from God and, indeed, it could be argued that such passive moments are crucial because they represent the height of one's encounter with the Spirit. But these encounters only make sense within the eschatological framework provided by the kingdom of God and its social expression through the Church. Within the fellowship of the body of Christ one can engage in evangelism and social action as well as prayer ministry and worship, all of which is wrapped in a famous prayer: 'Your kingdom come, your will be done, on earth as it is in heaven'. The kingdom of God signifies a taste of heaven, which is worth sharing with others for the glory of God.

7. THE COMMUNITY OF INTERPRETERS

Introduction

All Christian traditions throughout the history of the Church
have interpreted the Scriptures. For the early Church the
Scriptures were the Law, the Prophets and the Writings of the
Hebrew Bible. As the teachings of Jesus and the apostles were
written and circulated, so they came to be regarded as Scripture for the Church. Thus certain writings came to be recognised as functioning authoritatively within the community of
interpreters. Although there were disputes regarding the
composition of the canon, eventually authoritative books
received recognition. The actual process and details need not
concern us here. What is important is that a community of
interpreters existed throughout this process of textual transmission and reception. Clearly within the canon of Scripture,
there are indicators that the community of Israel, Jesus and
the Church are interpreting sacred texts that have been
written down in some fashion. In order to appreciate the ways
in which these communities have attempted to interpret
sacred texts, I shall briefly trace a trajectory from the Pentateuch through to the letter to the Hebrews. This description
provides a theological background to the manner in which the
charismatic tradition interprets the sacred text.

The book of Deuteronomy provides a good example of the
community of Israel interpreting the commandments of God
within the context of their shared life together. Moses is
recorded as instructing the people to be obedient to the
decrees and laws that have been revealed and taught

through him. They are to follow them in order that all may go well and they may dwell in the land. They are not to add to these laws nor to subtract from them but keep them (4:1-2). Thus the core teaching of the Ten Commandments forms the heart of this instruction and the basis of the covenant relationship established at Horeb (5:6-21). It is recorded that these commandments were written down on two stone tablets and were possessed as texts by the community. They are seen as instruction that can be passed down from generation to generation, as each embraces the covenant in order to enjoy long life in the land (6:2). However, the interpretation of these commandments is very much understood within a monotheistic faith, amidst the polytheism of the surrounding peoples, and as obedience that requires total commitment: 'Love the Lord your God with all your heart and with all your soul and with all your strength' (6:5). The commandments are to be impressed upon their hearts, on their children, to be talked about and to be bound symbolically on their foreheads, and even door-frames and gates (6:6-9). Thus love for the Lord is to be seen in the obedience to his decrees (11:1). Towards the end of the book, Moses is recorded as writing down the Law and giving it to the priests, and presumably this refers to laws other than the Ten Commandments, laws found in what we would call the Torah, or Pentateuch. He instructed them that they should come together (at the end of each seven-year period) during the Feast of Tabernacles and that the Law should be read before the people (31:9-13). Thus the people must be hearers of the laws of God.

This commitment to the Law of Moses is also seen in the response of King Josiah. In the second book of Kings (chs. 22–3; // 2 Chron. 34–5), Hilkiah discovers the Book of the Law during the temple's restoration and brings it to the secretary Shaphan, who, after reading it, brings it to King Josiah and reads it to him. The king reacts swiftly and asks the priests to enquire from the Lord regarding his attitude towards the people for their negligence of the Law. They enquire of the prophetess Huldah who delivers an oracle of judgement but not upon Josiah. In response Josiah calls the elders and leaders of Israel together in order to hear the Book of the Law read and renews the covenant in the presence of all the people as they pledge themselves again. As a consequence, altars to Baal and Asherah are destroyed, as is the shrine to Molech and chariots to the sun god. The Feast of the Passover is reinstated and mediums and spiritists, idols and household gods are rejected (2 Kgs. 23:24). These responses are recorded as reflecting Josiah's commitment to love the Lord with all his heart, soul and strength (2 Kgs. 23:25).

After the exile, when Israel had begun to return to Jerusalem, Ezra gathers the people and instructs them in the Law of Moses (Neh. 8:1). He reads the Law to an assembled crowd of all who are able to understand. Indeed, he reads it aloud from dawn until noon and all the people listen attentively to it. Nehemiah and Ezra instruct the people in the Law and it is a day of rejoicing (Neh. 8:9-10). The next day the heads of the families and the priests and Levites gather around the Book of the Law again. They discover instructions regarding the Festival of Booths and declare a commitment to it, thus the community celebrates the festival once again. During the feast, Ezra continues to read from the Book of the Law. Afterwards, the people repent for their failures, continue to read the Book of the Law for a quarter of the day and spend another quarter in confession and worship (Neh. 9:3). They are also reminded of their history as the story of the people of Israel from Abraham to Moses and the Promised Land, also including their rebellion and disobedience (Neh. 9:5-37). Towards the end of the book of Nehemiah, the Law of Moses is read and the exclusive nature of the people of Israel rediscovered in relation to foreigners (Neh. 13:1, 3). Thus the identity of the people is renewed.

From these passages it can be seen that the people of Israel from an early time wrote the laws of God down and these became the heart of the community's guidance for life in the land established by the covenant. It is also clear that the laws are wider than the Ten Commandments and probably included much of what we call the Torah, or the Pentateuch. However, it is worth noting that alongside the reading of the Law is often a narrative that summarises the story of Israel's establishment through the Patriarchs and Moses. This story of salvation also provides the community of interpreters with a framework for interpreting the Law of Moses. And this interpretation gives rise to celebration through festivals, again reminding the community of the story of salvation (e.g. the Passover).

In the New Testament, there is ample evidence that Jesus, as a son of the commandment, is one who interprets the Law, the Prophets and the Writings within the community of his day. In Matthew's Gospel, he teaches the Law on the Sermon on the Mount (5–7) and fulfils and goes beyond it. He also reinterprets certain commandments, such as the Sabbath since he is the Lord of the Sabbath (12.8). In Luke's Gospel he is found in the synagogue reading from the book of the prophet Isaiah (4:18-19; Isa. 61:1-2) and thus implicitly claiming messianic status. For the early Church, Jesus fulfils the promises of the prophets as God provides a new exodus liberation and this is now established by the work of his Spirit in the Church (Acts 2:14-39; Joel 2:28-32; Ps 16:8-11). At various points in the Acts of the Apostles the work of Jesus is interpreted in the light of Old Testament scriptures as fulfilling the promises of God to his people (7:1-53; 8:31-3; 15:15-18). Thus Paul can say that everything written in the Scriptures was written for our encouragement and hope (Rom. 15:4). This is because such testimony is inspired by God and profitable for the community of faith (2 Tim. 3:16). In the past God spoke through the patriarchs and the prophets but his final revelation has come through the Son, the heir of all things, through whom he made the universe (Heb. 1:1-2).

The community of interpreters in the New Testament takes on a different character. The Law is now fulfilled in the person of Jesus Christ, for he is the supreme revelation of

God. He is the *telos* (the end) of the Law (Rom. 10:4). The promises of God for the people of Israel are still important but Christ becomes the key by which these Old Testament scriptures are interpreted. Thus he fulfils the Law, the Prophets and the Writings and bestows his Spirit on his people to assist them in the interpretation of those Scriptures. There is still a narrative of God's saving power and mighty acts but this now includes the resurrection and exaltation of Christ and the bestowal of the Spirit at Pentecost. And still there are laws, but they now revolve around Christ and his kingdom, and are renewed as love of God and love of neighbour. Indeed, it is the Spirit of God who inspires the people of God to love him with all their heart, mind, soul and strength.

For Pentecostals and Charismatics the Bible is supremely important. In many respects they have an enormous amount in common with Evangelicals and others who have a high regard for the inspired nature of the text. However, they approach the text in a different manner to many other Christians who read the Bible seriously. In this chapter I aim to illustrate a description of biblical interpretation with respect to two strands of reading. The first arises from contemporary Pentecostal scholarship and is represented by two Americans, Kenneth Archer and John Christopher Thomas. The second arises from the world of the popular preacher and can be seen in the writings of the famous early twentieth-century Canadian evangelist and church leader Aimee Semple McPherson and the popular British writer, academic and Anglican priest Mark Stibbe. The first strand provides a broader approach to how the community of the Church interprets Scripture, while the second gives an illustration of how individual preachers have interpreted it charismatically in the light of their own contexts. I conclude by suggesting how these approaches can provide an 'interpretive centre' for the charismatic tradition.

Early and Contemporary Pentecostal Biblical Interpretation

Contemporary Pentecostals wish to place the authoritative text of Scripture firmly within the horizon of the contemporary Church. It is the corporate body of the Church that together interprets the text of Scripture and tests its practices of worship and witness. The Bible is believed to be a text inspired by the Spirit of God but it needs to be read with the continued inspiration of the Spirit within the community for it to be interpreted appropriately. Therefore, the inspiration is not simply codified within the words on a page, but made to live experientially because of the same Spirit who lives within the hearts of believers. It is therefore the focal point of God's continued acts of revelation today. This is because the text of Scripture is consciously interpreted within the context of the community and its life by means of 'ongoing' inspiration of the Spirit. To read the Bible is to engage in a 'sacred encounter' with the Spirit and, as such, enables experiences of God to occur. It is therefore the primary reference point for communion with God and provides a set of lenses through which to read the world.[1]

Kenneth Archer has argued that early Pentecostal biblical interpretation has its roots in the Holiness movements (Wesleyan and Keswick) of the nineteenth century and that it was a form of interpretation known simply as the 'Bible Reading Method'.[2] This approach was less concerned with constructing a systematic theology or discussing the exegetical details of the passages of Scripture and more concerned with living the Christian life in continuity with the 'Apostolic Faith'. It resulted in an expression of Christianity that was pietistic and practical, Jesus-centred with an emphasis upon discipleship. It was a commonsense method of interpretation that analysed the biblical material according to themes and then synthesised it on a particular subject, in this way providing a harmonised account. It was thus a modified form of the 'proof-text' approach to the biblical interpretation.[3]

Scripture was used to interpret Scripture in a coherent manner that did not focus on the historical and cultural context of the biblical texts and in that sense it was both popularist and 'pre-critical'.

This approach to the Bible, Archer contends, is best understood from a Pentecostal perspective as emerging out of a narrative community: so the Pentecostal community tells a shared story about its own identity as expressed in its 'shared charismatic experiences' and understanding of the 'Full Gospel' or 'Five-fold Gospel'.[4] As such it aims to embody a particular expression of the Christian story as an authentic restoration of New Testament Christianity to the contemporary world. In this dialogue between the scriptural story and the contemporary stories of the Pentecostal community the reading tradition is shaped and reshaped giving meaning to the interpretive community. The promise-fulfilment strategy of reading the narrative allowed for earlier promises to be fulfilled, including the promise of the Spirit to be poured out as 'Latter Rain' in anticipation of the second coming of Christ. This motif guided much of the early Pentecostal interpretation, as they interpreted their charismatic experiences as fulfilment of this promise.[5] Signs and wonders became authenticating evidence for the Pentecostal interpretation of the Christian story in the twentieth century. Thus 'experiential knowledge must be *revealed* by the Holy Spirit, *validated* by the Scriptures, and *confirmed* by the community'.[6] Archer bases this understanding on a fellow Pentecostal, although develops it, and it is to his colleague that I now turn.

John Christopher Thomas has articulated a useful example of how a Pentecostal theological method might work in relation to Acts 15 and the decision to include the Gentiles within the community of the early Church.[7] I refer to it in order to illustrate the kind of approach that is being proposed within contemporary Pentecostal scholarship.

The Jerusalem Council was convened in order to ascertain whether Gentile believers in Jesus should first convert to

Judaism in order to become Christians. The believers who were also Pharisees wanted to see Gentiles circumcised and obey the Law of Moses. In response, Peter notes what God had already done among the Gentiles: he allowed them to hear the gospel and believe; he had given them the Holy Spirit, and made no distinction between Jew and Gentile and purified their hearts by faith (vv. 7-9). Therefore to place the Law upon these Gentiles would in effect be a way of testing God (v. 10). It is through grace that people are saved (v. 11). Subsequently, Paul and Barnabas report all God has done among the Gentiles in terms of signs and wonders.

James addresses the Council and interprets Peter's account to mean that God has received the Gentiles as a people for his name (v. 14). This experience, he argues, is in line with Scripture, and so he cites Amos 9:11-12. In the light of this experience and its agreement with the prophets, the Gentiles should not have their lives made more difficult and be forced to observe the Law of Moses. Rather instructions should be modest: abstain from polluted foods, from the meat of strangled animals and from blood, and from sexual immorality. In verse 28 the decision is ascribed to 'the Holy Spirit and to us'.

Thomas makes a number of observations. The frequency to which the experience of the Church through the hand of God is appealed to in the discussion is significant. This unexpected move is attributed to the Holy Spirit. The Church begins with experience before moving to Scripture. Peter has concluded that even to question the place of the Gentiles within the Church is tantamount to testing God himself. Barnabas and Paul primarily discuss their experience of signs and wonders among the Gentiles and assume therefore that God had accepted them. James also supports this appeal to experience and lends the wider church community's support to the case. At this point Scripture is appealed to for the first time. Amos 9:11-12 seems to be used because it agrees with the experience of the Church. However, Thomas asks about the original meaning of this passage. The Pharisees

could have appealed to other texts for an exclusive position
on this issue (Exod. 19:5; Deut. 7:6; 14:2; 26:18-19). James
appears to follow the Septuagint's more inclusive rendering
of the Masoretic Text. But why choose this particular text?
Other texts could support this position better (Isa. 2:3; 42:6;
Mic. 4:2; and Zech. 2:11). The answer, for Thomas, lies with
the redactional intention of Luke. He is concerned to
demonstrate that the promises made to David are fulfilled in
Jesus and that they have implications for the Church (Luke
1:27; 1:32-3; 1:69; 2:4; 2:11; 3:31; 6:3; 18:38-9; 20:41-4; Acts
1:16; 2:25-8; 2:29-36; 4:25; 7:45-6; 13:22-3; 13:34; 13:36). Luke
is concerned to demonstrate the continuity between David
and Jesus. The citing of the rebuilding of David's fallen tent
conveys the notion of the expansion as well as the restoration
of the house of Israel. Although James has the authority to
pronounce the decision, the process of decision-making
involved the whole group (15:24-6). The stipulations do not
include circumcision, but do include food laws and sexual
morality. The food laws are puzzling in the light of later
church practice. Thomas suggests that perhaps they are best
seen as temporary and transitional steps to ensure table
fellowship. Later they appeared to be disregarded.

From this passage, Thomas discerns three key components
in a theological method. These include the role of the community, which gathers together in order to give and receive
testimony and assess the reports. Luke also regards the
decision-making process to be directed by the Holy Spirit,
both in terms of the action of God among the Gentiles and in
enabling the community to make a decision. The text of
Scripture is used but in an unusual way by today's stan-
dards. The community moved from context to text, and the
experience of the Spirit seems to be a factor in the selection
and appropriation of the text. From this example, we can
suggest that the method amounts to a text-community-Spirit
model and this, Thomas maintains, has much in common
with the contemporary Pentecostal method of biblical interpretation. He proposes a number of features. (1) The

Pentecostal method has a basis in Scripture itself. (2) The community functions as a place where the Spirit acts, where testimony is given and assessed, and is a forum for discussion, accountability and support. (3) The explicit dependence on the Holy Spirit in the process is greater than mere 'illumination'. The Holy Spirit creates the context for interpretation, guides the Church in the selection of texts and clarifies how best they should be used. (4) The text is not static but dynamic and demands a more intensive engagement in order to discover its truths. (5) Scripture is clearly regarded as authoritative, and the Church must measure its practices and views against it, but allowing the form and content of the canon to define the nature of its authority. (6) This paradigm could assist the Church in contentious issues of today.

Therefore, the negotiation of meaning takes seriously the contribution of the biblical text, the contribution of the Pentecostal reading community using a narrative method and the contributions of the Holy Spirit via Scripture and the voices in the community.[8] This triad *cannot* be separated and together enables the tradition to be renewed in its worship and life.

'This is That' Interpretation

One aspect of this hermeneutic that has been picked up by the charismatic tradition is the way in which the biblical horizons merge into the contemporary ones: the experiences of the early Christians are being repeated in a different time and place. This can be seen in the writings of two preachers.

The first is in the work of the famous evangelist and preacher Aimee Semple McPherson, who founded the denomination called the Church of the Foursquare Gospel.[9] In 1923 she published a book containing a mixture of testimonies, accounts of her many revivals, some diary entries and a number of sermons. The fundamental theme of the book is provided by the text of Acts 2:16-18: 'This is that

which was spoken by the prophet Joel: "And it shall come to
pass in the last days, says God, I will pour out my Spirit
upon all flesh; and your sons and daughters shall prophesy...
and upon my servants and my handmaidens I will pour out,
in those days, of my Spirit; and they shall prophesy"' [KJV].
The various accounts of her experience of coming to faith,
baptism in the Spirit, call to Christian ministry and her
evangelistic and Pentecostal camps testify to this theme. The
God of the Bible, of Pentecost, is the same now as then and
the fact is demonstrated in the notion that the 'this' of present experience is the 'that' of the experience of the Pentecost
church. That which was spoken of by the prophet Joel has
come to pass in these last days.

The different testimonies are accounts of how the Pentecost
message has come to be preached in North America and the
ways in which various groups of people, from young to old,
rich to poor and White to Black, have come to embrace the
Pentecost experience as the same as the biblical experience.
As an example of her willingness to speak of her gospel, the
words from the following account give a flavour of her
thinking and speech:

> The Lord put such a love in my heart for the coloured race
> that it was almost impossible for me to pass one of them on
> the street without such floods of love welling up in my
> heart that I had to step up to them and inquire: 'Have you
> heard of the latter rain outpouring of the Holy Ghost, the
> baptism of the Holy Ghost, and of the soon coming of
> Jesus?'[10]

Indeed the preaching of Pentecost was in terms of a four-fold
gospel message: 'Salvation by faith, healing for the body, the
baptism of the Holy Spirit and the glorious imminent coming of
the Lord Jesus'.[11] Thus the experience of salvation, healing and
baptism in the Spirit represent a preparation for the second
coming of Christ as the promise of Joel is fulfilled in the latter
rain outpouring. These gospel themes are supported by the
community of Pentecostals as well as individual experiences.

One example of how she read the Bible through an experiential and pneumatological lens is provided in her sermon on Ezekiel 37:1-14 and the vision of dry bones.[12] In this sermon she takes phrases from the account and applies each to her own ministry. Thus, for example, the phrase 'The hand of the Lord was upon me', she immediately uses in relation to her work in Florida. She too has felt the hand of the Lord upon her and setting her down in a certain place and discovering that it is also a valley full of 'bones'. Each verse of this passage is reflected upon experientially as the account of the vision is brought to bear on experiences and vice versa. But at the point where Ezekiel prophesies to the bones, there is a clear correspondence with the falling of the power of the Holy Spirit so that men and women cry out to God: 'What shall I do to inherit eternal life and receive the Holy Spirit?'[13]

Three distinct things occurred in Ezekiel's vision that can be seen as corresponding to aspects of the contemporary revival of her day. First, there is noise as the Spirit moves upon the dry bones. This is linked to the latter rain of the Spirit which began to fall all over the world from 1907: 'Believers were filled with the Spirit, shouted, and often talked for hours at a time in tongues (Acts 2.4) as the Spirit gave utterance'.[14] Second, the first noise is followed by a rattling of the bones, associated with the shaking as factions within churches are displayed because the Spirit shakes, sifts and purges individuals and communities. Third, the bones come together and this is associated with a new-found unity between believers as the Spirit binds people with cords of love. 'This movement, please God, will never be one great *organization*, but rather an *Organism*. We *are* expecting, however, a unity amongst the different members of the body (such as we have never seen before) to develop right down here in this old world.'[15]

In the Ezekiel vision this is followed by the breath of the Spirit entering the bones, which again is linked to the promise of a personal Pentecost:

Oh if there is a soul here tonight who was once a dried-up skeleton, has now been redeemed and has been covered with the sinews and flesh and skin (the covering of grace and salvation), and you have been slain by the mighty word of his power, what you need now is the baptism of the Holy Spirit. The same Holy Spirit that filled the house with the sound as of a rushing, mighty wind on the day of Pentecost, shall come upon you, endue you with power, stand you upon your feet, and join you to this exceeding great army. (Rev 7.9)[16]

Whoever the listener may be, he or she is invited to receive salvation and the filling of the Spirit that will lead them to the Promised Land. These things are known by and through personal experience.

The second example is from a contemporary scholar who has also appropriated a similar approach, although in a more limited way and from a Third Wave (or perhaps Fourth Wave?) perspective. Mark Stibbe illustrates how a charismatic interpretation of the prophetic writings in Scripture also arises from the horizon of contemporary experience of the Spirit. His hermeneutical reflections on the interpretation of Ezekiel 47 were prompted by a colleague's charismatic interpretation of the passage in light of his experience of the Toronto Blessing.[17] He argues that the New Testament preachers and authors use the Hebrew Scriptures as a means of interpreting what God is doing in their midst right now, so they aim to find biblical passages that illuminate their experience. He calls this hermeneutic a 'this-is-that' approach. It starts with the 'this' that God is currently doing with his people and with the guidance of the Holy Spirit before attending to the 'that' in Scripture which explains what is happening. So in Acts 2:16 when Peter explains what has happened to the 120 on the Day of Pentecost, he says: 'This is that which was spoken by the prophet Joel' (KJV). Thus the 'primary task of exegesis involves us perceiving what the Father is doing right now among us (like Jesus in

John 5.19) and then allowing the Holy Spirit to lead us to Bible texts which elucidate that work'.[18] It is a form of contextualised hermeneutics whereby the communal story of the Church is understood in the light of the overarching story of Scripture.

The vision of Ezekiel 47:1-12 is one passage that has been interpreted in this way as the promise of renewal for Israel is applied to the Church today. From out of the Temple flow four waves: the first is ankle-deep, the second is knee-deep, the third is waist-high and the fourth is too deep to cross. These waves are interpreted symbolically as movements of the Holy Spirit. The fourth wave is the one that completes the process of renewal. The four waves are interpreted as a pattern for renewal both in the New Testament, with the application to the missionary movements of Acts (1:8): Jerusalem, Judea, Samaria and the whole earth, and for today. The thesis that Stibbe proposes is that the four 'waves' represent a 'this' corresponding to a 'that' found in Ezekiel 47:1-12. The waves are: (1) the emergence of Pentecostalism in 1906; (2) the emergence of the Charismatic Renewal in the early 1960s; (3) the emergence of Protestant Evangelical renewal in the early 1980s (sometimes called the 'Third Wave'); and (4) the Toronto Blessing signalling the coming of the fourth wave.

This approach has been criticised for allowing the postmodern 'playfulness' (i.e. viewing texts in many and varied ways without giving priority to any one interpretation) with regard to reading to have influenced Stibbe's exegesis.[19] In a response to the critique of John Lyons, and based upon an exegesis of Peter's speech in Acts 2, Stibbe argues that he has attempted to mediate between the conservative (original meaning of the text) approach and the postmodern (reader response approach).[20] His approach is neither one nor the other but both. He believes that a charismatic hermeneutic should be based on a 'rich harmony' between the text of Scripture and the present experience. This is followed by a 'this-is-that' dynamic by which analogies are used from the meta-narrative of Scripture. It is a reading that is achieved corporately since the Church is involved and it is undertaken within and for a community of faith. It is also centred round the person of Jesus Christ and his return. Cognition and affection are both engaged because emotional intelligence is recognised. Finally, this kind of reading is orientated towards praxis because there are important practical outcomes. In many ways this approach has much in common with the text-community-Spirit model outlined above and fits its contours.

Conclusion

The community of interpreters will inevitably vary because of time and place and in a sense the concept of 'community' is somewhat fluid. Nevertheless, there are groups of worshippers who gather together, who belong to denominations or networks, perhaps even international communions. In that sense there are many different levels of community organised in many different ways. What is important and what is intended by the concept of community in this particular form is the idea that Christians belong to one another and that there is a mutual responsibility and accountability for their interpretations and actions. Communities enable individuals to be in relations with others for the benefit of all. By its very nature Christianity has a social dynamic since it is about the people of God for the world.

Given the importance of the notion of community for Church and society, the charismatic tradition in its most recent expression seeks to give a renewed primacy to the role of the community for the interpretation of its life in practice. Therefore the community is regarded as the place where a 'spirituality of the Spirit' is located. It is the place and inter-personal relational context where individuals encounter the person of the Spirit in love and power. It is the place that guards and guides the spirituality process of search, encounter and transformation. It is also the place where the text of Scripture and the narrative of the charismatic tradition are interpreted experientially in ways that correlate the two, thus enabling participants to understand the meaning of the symbols and the praxis via the biblical narrative and *vice versa*. The key themes of the charismatic tradition find expression in community as it engages in praise and worship, inspired speech, holiness of life and empowered kingdom witness.

If Scripture is read by participants within the community who are active participants in the charismatic tradition, then a number of features will emerge. They will find meaning in the process, framework and themes of the spirituality. It will make sense to them over the course of time. They might use these themes alongside other aspects of the Christian tradition, but if this tradition has any dominant place then they will 'read' Scripture experientially as well as in other ways. It will begin to inform their worldview as the spirituality categories of narrative, symbols and praxis charismatically framed become more deeply embedded in their lives. For this to become 'second nature' some form of socialisation period will be required not just for the initial assimilation and appreciation of this spirituality but for continued engagement with it. This will be easier for those who are members of established Pentecostal or charismatic churches, since the distinctive features of the spirituality will be celebrated each week. The establishment of broader networks and annual events also provide support and resources for the charismatic tradition in order that it might be expressed and sustained across denominational affiliations.

CONCLUSION

Summary

The charismatic tradition is a strand of Christianity that stresses the role of the Holy Spirit, and in particular 'encounters' with the Spirit in a variety of ways. This idea is the key motif for the tradition and means of identifying its presence in historical and contemporary sources. I have suggested that this spirituality is given shape by considering it in terms of a process and a framework. The process is a cyclical one of searching for God, encountering him and being transformed by him for his purposes and glory. The agent of this process is God's Spirit. The spirituality can also be understood as a framework of narrative, symbols and praxis as each gives expression to a coherent worldview in which the Spirit of God is understood, symbolised and participated in. In this context there are key themes stressed by the tradition, namely: praise and worship, inspired speech, holiness and empowered kingdom witness. All of these themes are interpreted by the Christian community for the sake of its identity and life. In addition, it can be seen that aspects of this tradition have been displayed throughout the history of the Church. These aspects have been played out differently at various times and places but these themes are common and indicate its presence.

A number of metaphors can be used to attempt to understand the ways in which this tradition has been active throughout the history of the Church, and indeed how it is played out today. The first is the metaphor of 'plug 'n' play', taken from the use of electrical instruments or devices.[1] In this sense, the tradition can plug into and be played along-side other traditions. This is probably a more suitable metaphor for describing some of the charismatic renewal movements where it is expressed within the structures of another tradition rather than creating its own structures. However, this metaphor can appear mechanical or automatic and the notion of 'plugging in' can have its limitations. The second metaphor is the 'infusion' of different flavours in the culinary process. Here the flavour of the charismatic tradi-tion influences and permeates other traditions. It is in the mix, being distinct and yet cannot be separated from other traditions. In a sense the charismatic tradition's relation to Evangelicalism in contemporary Christianity is perhaps a good example of this. Often there is an infusion of one in and with the other. Third, there is the metaphor of a stream or river that flows through the landscape and brings life and vitality to the land. In this topographical metaphor there is one main source of life, namely the Spirit of God. The char-ismatic tradition would see itself as a witness to this source of spiritual life as a challenge to exclusively formal expres-sions of Christianity. Of course, like all metaphors these vary in their applicability and usefulness, and their suitability will need to be tested in relation to specific and global expressions of the tradition.

Strengths and Weakness of the Tradition in Contemporary Expression

It is inevitable that Christian spiritual traditions have strengths and weaknesses, or bring insights and contain blind-spots. As a way of offering a brief evaluation, in conclusion I mention some areas for further reflection by those embracing this tradition. In this evaluation I am considering the tradition in its contemporary form. Some of these points have already been mentioned in earlier chapters.

The charismatic tradition has a good number of strengths and a few are worth noting here.

First, there is the ability to give a full expression to the importance of experience. Of course, it is experience within certain parameters and interpreted in particular ways, but it enables individuals and groups to connect Christianity to their everyday lives. As such it is holistic, uniting the affective and the cognitive dimensions together in purposeful action. It overcomes the old dualisms in Western thought (e.g. body and spirit) and allows people once again to connect their faith to all areas of their existence. A considerable amount of Christian expression can appear to be dull and lifeless. The charismatic tradition emphasises the engagement of God with people that connects to an experiential reality that is vibrant.

Second, there is the openness to the empowering of *all* of God's people, whatever the socio-economic and educational differences, because the Spirit is no respecter of persons. Therefore there is a radical egalitarianism in the Spirit that transcends different boundaries in releasing gifts and ministries. This means that whatever the background or location of individuals they may be used by God in his service. Ministry is no longer limited to the professional and the elite but belongs to the whole body of Christ. Every member of that body can potentially engage in ministry, bringing gifts and talents to use for the benefit of all.

Third, in theological terms, the Cinderella of theology, the doctrine of the Holy Spirit, has finally been allowed to attend the ball. Instead of being ignored or being subordinated to other persons, the third person of the Trinity is beginning to be appreciated once again. A fully robust Trinitarian theology is being developed that is biblical and theologically aware. This rediscovery of the theology of the Holy Spirit has also been accompanied by an increasingly sophisticated approach to theology by Pentecostal and Charismatic theologians. The effect of such a recovery of the Spirit is not just a renewal in the doctrine of the Trinity but also in many other areas of theology, such as ecclesiology and mission.

There are also weaknesses and it is important to try and

identify these. Again, I mention three areas, although I know there are more.

First, with the emphasis on power and the immediacy of the transcendent within the immanent, the charismatic tradition can err on the side of expecting too much now. This is what theologians call the problem of 'over-realised eschatology'. The kingdom of God is perceived to be here in its fullness, which is a similar belief to the super-spiritual elite of the Corinthian church addressed by Paul. The power of the resurrection can eclipse the weakness of the cross and this can be played out in the life of the tradition as a whole. Success and celebrity status can be sought as signs of power and blessing rather than a commitment to suffering and weakness in the ordinary of everyday life. The mystery that surrounds suffering in this world can often be explained through 'lack of faith' or 'lack of power' and this can result in poor pastoral care.

Second, as mentioned earlier, the category of creation or nature can be lost in a worldview that sees reality in the dichotomous terms of light and darkness, or the spiritual kingdom of God versus the spiritual kingdom of Satan. This cosmological dualism can fuel spiritual warfare, but it also misses the important category of creation as good but fallen. Spiritual warfare need not be denied (and I would not wish to do so) in order to include this third category and it would enable the tradition to be slightly more world-affirming than world-denying. Such discernment would enable a greater engagement in society and a willingness to work alongside others for the transformation of social structures whilst being aware that ultimately the kingdom of God is what matters.

Third, while I might extol the virtues of a charismatically renewed scholarly guild, I know that the relationship of it to popular piety is variable. In some places the impact of mature and wise theological thinking is distinctly lacking and this means that odd ideas are taught and often a cult of the personality results. Popular preachers in the charismatic tradition can exhibit enormous influence and yet lack any sense of responsibility to the broader theological tradition and the universal Church. There is a 'wacky' side to the tradition that has often been marginalised and understandably so. However, a greater engagement is required by Pentecostal and charismatic theological educators and this is a matter of urgency in some situations.

Every spiritual tradition has its limitations and it is often only in dialogue with other traditions that insights and blindspots are identified. Positively, I wish to affirm this tradition as an 'insider', as a charismatic Anglican, but I do believe that it needs to engage in this dialogue with others. As I have offered a brief evaluation of the charismatic tradition in its contemporary expression, I would invite you to do the same with your own preferred tradition, whatever that might be and however you might wish to define it.

An Invitation: 'Come, Holy Spirit!'

In this book the charismatic tradition has been elucidated in terms of a central motif: 'encountering the Spirit'. For many Christians throughout the centuries the desire to encounter the presence of the living and triune God by the person of his Spirit has been expressed in song and prayer. This is true for both the Western and Eastern traditions. As a way of concluding this account of the charismatic spiritual tradition, I would like to allow the words of one theologian from the tenth and eleventh century to stand as a testimony to it. Symeon the New Theologian, as I have already described him in chapter 2, is a significant figure in the Eastern tradition, and some of his words have a timeless quality to them. They could be sung to different kinds and styles of music from various historical and cultural locations. The following words belong to an invitation in prayer for the Spirit to come. I suggest that if you feel able, you read, ponder and pray them for yourself.

Invocation to the Holy Spirit, by the one who already sees him.

Come, true light.
Come, eternal life.
Come, hidden mystery.
Come, nameless treasure.
Come, ineffable reality.
Come, inconceivable person.
Come, endless bliss.
Come, non-setting sun.
Come, infallible expectation of those who must be saved.
Come, awakening of those who are asleep.
Come, resurrection of the dead.
Come, O Powerful One, who always creates and recreates and transforms by your will alone.
Come, O invisible and totally intangible and impalpable.
Come, you who always remain motionless and at each moment move completely and come to us...
Come, O beloved Name and repeated everywhere...
Come, eternal joy.
Come, non-tarnishing crown.
Come, purple of the great king our God.
Come, crystalline cincture, studded with precious stones.
Come, inaccessible sandal.
Come, royal purple.
Come, truly sovereign right hand.
Come, you whom my miserable soul has desired and desires.
Come, you the Lonely, to the lonely, since you see I am lonely...
Come, you who have become yourself desire in me, who have made my desire you...
Come, my breath and my life.
Come, consolation of my poor soul.
Come, my joy, my glory, my endless delight.[2]

It is my prayer that this tradition may be appreciated for what it is and that all God's people may seek and encounter, and thus be transformed by, the Spirit of triune God, who is the Spirit of Christ, to the glory of his name.

NOTES

1. Charismatic Spirituality

1. Walter J. Hollenweger, *Pentecostalism: Origins and Developments Worldwide* (Peabody MA: Hendrickson, 1997), p. 2. Other historians, e.g. Neil Hudson, would contest this reading of Pentecostal origins with respect to the UK. Hudson would argue that British Pentecostalism owes more to its Wesleyan Holiness heritage than African religious roots and that this Holiness tradition contained all the necessary elements for an emergent Pentecostalism. I am grateful for his comment on this matter.

2. The origin of Pentecostalism is a matter of scholarly debate. American historiography is now disputed as biased, ignoring revivals elsewhere in the world around the same time, e.g. the Welsh Revival (1904–5), as well as revivals in South India (1860), North East India (1905), Pune, India (Mukti Mission, 1905–6), and in Korea (1907–8).

3. Hollenweger, *Pentecostalism*, pp. 18–19.

4. Allan Anderson, *An Introduction to Pentecostalism: Global Charismatic Christianity* (Cambridge: Cambridge University Press, 2004), p. 34.

5. See Andrew Walker, *Restoring the Kingdom: The Radical Christianity of the House Church Movement,* 2nd edn (London: Hodder & Stoughton, 1988).

6. 'Introduction' in S.M. Burgess and E.M. Van der Mass (eds.), *The New International Dictionary of Pentecostal and Charismatic Movements – Revised and Expanded Edition* (Grand Rapids: Zondervan, 2002), p. xx.

7. Alistair E. McGrath, *Christian Spirituality* (Oxford: Blackwell, 1999), p. 2.

8. See Mark A. McIntosh, *Mystical Theology* (Oxford: Blackwell, 1998), pp. 3–34.

9. *ibid.*, pp. 5–6.

10. N.T. Wright, *The New Testament and the People of God,* 2nd edn (London: SPCK, 1993), p. 124.

11. Jackie D. Johns, 'Pentecostalism and the Postmodern Worldview', *Journal of Pentecostal Theology* 7 (1995), pp. 73–96, suggests that, for Pentecostals, Scripture is a living book in which the Holy Spirit is

active and through which God is encountered. Therefore, Scripture functions (1) as a primary reference point for communion with God; (2) as a template for reading the world; and (3) as a link to God's people and God's presence in the world and throughout the ages (p. 90).

12. Steven J. Land, *Pentecostal Spirituality: A Passion for the Kingdom* (Sheffield: Sheffield Academic Press, JPTSup 1, 1993), pp. 74–5.

13. *ibid.*, p. 75.

14. John Goldingay, 'Charismatic Spirituality: Some Theological Reflections', *Theology* 789 (1996), pp. 178–87, esp. pp. 181–2, offers a typology from a charismatic perspective which sees God's action in the world in terms of (1) the miraculous, (2) interaction, (3) cause and effect, and (4) human decisions. I think that categories (3) and (4) could also be defined in terms of interaction. See my categorisation in M.J. Cartledge, 'A Spur to Holistic Discipleship', in *'Toronto' in Perspective*, ed. by D. Hilborn (Carlisle: Evangelical Alliance/ Paternoster, 2001), pp. 64–71.

15. Simon Chan, *Pentecostal Theology and the Christian Spiritual Tradition* (Sheffield: Sheffield Academic Press, JPTSup 21, 2000), p. 118, understandably criticises the pragmatic reason for worship which is so prevalent in charismatic thinking. But this need not be the case.

16. For a review of recent scholarship on the subject, plus my own perspective, see M.J. Cartledge, *Charismatic Glossolalia: An Empirical-Theological Study* (Aldershot: Ashgate, 2002).

17. Walter J. Hollenweger, *Geist und Materie* (Muenchen: Chr. Kaiser Verlag, 1988, Interkulturelle Theologie 3), pp. 314–15, cited by F.D. Macchia, 'Tongues as a Sign: Toward a Sacramental Understanding of Pentecostal Experience', *PENUMA: The Journal of the Society for Pentecostal Studies* 15.1 (1993), pp. 61–76 (p. 61).

18. D.E. Albrecht, *Rites in the Spirit: A Ritual Approach to Pentecostal/ Charismatic Spirituality* (Sheffield: Sheffield Academic Press, JPTS 17, 1999), p. 216, writes: 'The desire for transformation drives nearly all Pent/Char ritual. This desire appears in the language and other symbols of Pentecostal ritual. Transformation symbols that permeate the rites, the testimonies, the songs, the sermonic illustrations and the altar calls, to name a few, express the language of transformation.'

19. One person who has argued that speaking in tongues should be linked to issues of social change from a Black Pentecostal liberationist perspective is R. Beckford, 'Back to my roots: speaking in tongues for a new *ecclesia*', *TransMission* (Bible Society, summer 2000), pp. 12–13. See also R. Beckford, *Dread and Pentecostal: A Political Theology for the Black Church in Britain* (London: SPCK, 2000).

20. Land, *Pentecostal Spirituality*, p. 166.

21. My research has suggested that extrovert women more than men are

attracted by charismatic spirituality, see *Charismatic Glossolalia*, ch. 5. For a review of women's ministry in terms of prophecy see M.J. Cartledge, *Practical Theology: Charismatic and Empirical Perspectives* (Carlisle: Paternoster, 2003), pp. 157–74.

22. It is interesting to note that the first booklet in the Grove Renewal series is on this subject because of its importance. See John Leech, *Developing Prayer Ministry: A New Introduction for Churches* (Cambridge: Grove Books Ltd, 2000).

2. The Charismatic Tradition in Church History

1. I have used two main Pentecostal sources for this historical sketch. The first is by Stanley M. Burgess, and is a trilogy examining material relating to the Holy Spirit in the Early, Eastern and Western Churches: *The Holy Spirit: Ancient Christian Traditions* (Peabody MA: Hendrickson, 1984); *The Holy Spirit: Eastern Christian Traditions*, 2nd edn (Peabody, MA: Hendrickson, 1993); and *The Holy Spirit: Medieval Roman Catholic and Reformation Traditions* (Peabody, MA: Hendrickson, 1997). In effect, Burgess's survey provides a framework for this chapter. A second source is David Allen, *The Unfailing Stream: A Charismatic Church History in Outline* (Tonbridge: Sovereign World, 1994).

2. Burgess, *The Holy Spirit: Ancient Christian Traditions*, p. 3, suggests that major theologians have marginalised pneumatology because of an emphasis on soteriology and an impression that Charismatics were attempting to domesticate the divine.

3. A Pentecostal and Charismatic Timeline is provided by Stanley M. Burgess and Eduard M. Van Der Mass (eds.) in *The New International Dictionary of Pentecostal and Charismatic Movements – Revised and Expanded Edition* (Grand Rapids: Zondervan, 2002), pp. 1227–34.

4. Allan Anderson, *An Introduction to Pentecostalism: Global Charismatic Christianity* (Cambridge: Cambridge University Press, 2004), pp. 19–25, offers a similar sketch based on the work of Burgess in Burgess and Van Der Mass (eds.), *The New International Dictionary of Pentecostal and Charismatic Movements*.

5. See, for example, the *Didache* 11.7–12, and the commentary by A. Milacev, *The Didache: Text, Analysis and Commentary* (Minnesota: Liturgical Press, 2003), pp. 29, 69–76.

6. Burgess, *The Holy Spirit: Ancient Traditions*, p. 63.

7. C. White, *Early Christian Lives* (London: Penguin, 1998), pp. 3–70 (p. 44).

8. Burgess, *The Holy Spirit: Medieval Roman Catholic and Reformation Traditions*, p. 19.

9. Allen, *The Unfailing Stream*, p. 36.

10. Burgess, *The Holy Spirit: Eastern Christian Traditions*, p. 60.

11. See Fiona Bowie and Oliver Davies (eds.), *Hildegard of Bingen*, trans. by Robert Carver (London: SPCK, 1990); cf. Allen, *The Unfailing Stream*, pp. 38–41.
12. Allen, *The Unfailing Stream*, pp. 42–4.
13. Burgess, *The Holy Spirit: Medieval Roman Catholic and Reformation Traditions*, pp. 83–4.
14. *ibid.,* p. 149.
15. See P. Matheson (ed. and tr.), *The Collected Works of Thomas Müntzer* (Edinburgh: T & T Clark, 1988).
16. For a brief introduction see Peter Tyler, 'Alumbrados' in Philip Sheldrake (ed.), *The New SCM Dictionary of Christian Spirituality* (London: SCM-Canterbury, 2005), pp. 102–3 (I am grateful to Peter Tyler for a copy of this item); for fuller treatment see A. Hamilton, *Heresy and Mysticism in Sixteenth Century Spain: the Alumbrados* (Cambridge: James Clarke, 1992).
17. O.E. Winslow (ed.), *Jonathan Edwards: Basic Writings* (London: The New English Library, 1966), pp. 86–7.
18. There are many recorded reactions to his preaching, including one account by Sarah Ryan, 'An Account of a Woman of Long and Deep Experience', *The Arminian Magazine: For the Year 1779 Consisting of Extracts and Original Treatises on Universal Redemption,* vol. 2 (April 1754), pp. 296–309.
19. Allen, *The Unfailing Stream*, p. 72.
20. *ibid.*, pp. 80–93; for a detailed appraisal of Irving, see Gordon Strachan, *The Pentecostal Theology of Edward Irving* (Peabody, MA: Henrickson, 1973).
21. Michael Harper is the clearest and most significant example of this, see: *The True Light: An Evangelical's Journey to Orthodoxy* (London: Hodder & Stoughton, 1997). He maintains that Orthodoxy is charismatic and has always accepted the gifts of the Spirit in the life of the Church.

3. Praise and Worship

1. Daniel E. Albrecht, 'An Anatomy of Worship: A Pentecostal Analysis', in Wonsuk Ma and Robert P. Menzies (eds.), *The Spirit and Spirituality: Essays in Honour of Russell P. Spittler* (London: T & T Clark, JPTSup 24, 2004), pp. 70–82, identifies the values (experience, biblical authority, oral liturgy, spontaneity, spiritual gifts, ministry and mission), expressions (rites and acts) and sensibilities (embodied attitudes) that inform Pentecostal worship.
2. A.E. Dyer, 'Worship' in William K. Kay and Anne E. Dyer (eds.), *Pentecostal and Charismatic Studies: A Reader* (London: SCM, 2004), pp. 144–66 (p. 145).
3. Walter J. Hollenweger, *Pentecostalism: Origins and Developments Worldwide* (Peabody MA: Hendrickson, 1997), p. 271.

4. Harvey Cox, *Fire From Heaven: The Rise of Pentecostal Spirituality and the Reshaping of Religion in the Twenty-First Century* (London: Cassell, 1996), pp. 139–57, makes a fascinating comparison of Pentecostal worship and jazz. He also regards charismatic renewal as a toned-down version of the real Pentecostal thing, primly packaged 'without blue notes, drum breaks and gut-bucket choruses' (p. 152).
5. Jean-Jacques Suurmond, *Word and Spirit at Play: Towards a Charismatic Theology* (London: SCM, 1994), p. 59.
6. James H.S. Steven, *Worship in the Spirit: Charismatic Worship in the Church of England* (Carlisle: Paternoster, 2002), pp. 91–134.
7. This is also noted by Robin Parry, *Worshipping Trinity: Coming Back to the Heart of Worship* (Milton Keynes: Paternoster, 2005), pp. 139–46.
8. Steven, *Worship in the Spirit*, p. 118.
9. *ibid.*, p. 127.
10. Hollenweger, *Pentecostalism*, p. 278.
11. D.L. Alford, 'Music, Pentecostal and Charismatic', in S.M. Burgess and E.M. Van Der Mass (eds.), *The New International Dictionary of Pentecostal and Charismatic Movements – Expanded and Revised Edition* (Grand Rapids: Zondervan, 2002), p. 914.
12. An interesting comparison of charismatic and Methodist hymnody is suggested by James H.S. Steven, 'Charismatic Hymnody in the Light of Early Methodist Hymnody', *Studia Liturgia* 27.2 (1997), pp. 217–34.
13. D. Neil Hudson, 'Worship: Singing a New Song in a Strange Land', in Keith Warrington (ed.), *Pentecostal Perspectives* (Carlisle: Paternoster, 1998), pp. 177–203 (p. 183).
14. Nigel Scotland, *Charismatics and the Next Millennium: Do They Have a Future?* (London: Hodder & Stoughton, 1995), p. 56; Steven, 'Charismatic Hymnody', pp. 217–18.
15. Alford, 'Music, Pentecostal and Charismatic', p. 918.
16. Victoria Cooke, *Understanding Songs in Renewal* (Cambridge: Grove Books Ltd, R4, 2001), p. 13.
17. *ibid.*, pp. 4–5.
18. J. Begbie, 'The Spirituality of Renewal Music: A Preliminary Exploration', *Anvil: An Anglican Evangelical Journal for Theology and Mission* 8.3 (1991), pp. 227–39 (pp. 231–2).
19. These two points have been made by Begbie, 'The Spirituality of Renewal Music', pp. 232–3.
20. Pete Ward, 'Affective Alliance or Circuits of Power: The Production and Consumption of Contemporary Charismatic Worship in Britain', *International Journal of Practical Theology* 9 (2005), pp. 25–39.

4. Inspired Speech

1. Mark J. Cartledge, 'Charismatic Prophecy: A Definition and Description', *Journal of Pentecostal Theology* 5 (1994), pp. 79–120.
2. John Wimber, *Power Evangelism: Signs and Wonders Today* (London: Hodder & Stoughton, 1985), p. 44.
3. Bruce Yocum, *Prophecy* (Ann Arbor: Servant Books, 1976), p. 75.
4. Joyce Huggett, *Listening to God* (London: Hodder & Stoughton, 1986), p. 98.
5. Barry Kissell, *Walking on Water* (London: Hodder & Stoughton, 1987), p. 44.
6. For a more detailed discussion of this subject, see the following: Mark J. Cartledge, *The Gift of Speaking in Tongues: The Holy Spirit, the Human Spirit and the Gift of Holy Speech* (Cambridge: Grove Books, R 19, 2005). And for more detailed academic treatment, see Mark J. Cartledge, *Charismatic Glossolalia: An Empirical-theological Study* (Aldershot: Ashgate, 2002); also Mark J. Cartledge (ed.), *Speaking in Tongues: Multi-disciplinary Perspectives* (Carlisle: Paternoster, 2006).
7. Walter J. Hollenweger, *The Pentecostals: The Charismatic Movement in the Churches* (London: SCM, 1972), p. 344.
8. Cartledge, *Speaking in Tongues* (2005), pp. 15–17.
9. Perhaps one of the most significant influences in this regard has been the book by Wayne Grudem, *The Gift of Prophecy* (Eastbourne: Kingsway, 1988).
10. 'Reading Prophecy', *Renewal* 64 (1976), p. 19.
11. Douglas McBain, *Eyes that See* (Basingstoke: Marshall Pickering, 1981), p. 5.
12. For a sophisticated proposal of spiritual discernment, see Amos Yong, 'Spiritual Discernment: A Biblical-Theological Reconsideration' in Wonsuk Ma and Robert P. Menzies (eds.), *The Spirit and Spirituality: Essays in Honour of Russell P. Spittler* (London: T & T Clark, JPTSup 24, 2004), pp. 83–107.
13. One of the most famous Pentecostal preachers was Aimee Semple McPhearson, whose highly dramatic style attracted many visitors, see Edith L. Blumhofer, *Aimee Semple McPherson: Everybody's Sister* (Grand Rapids: Eerdmans, 1993), pp. 258–62.
14. Mark J. Cartledge, *Testimony: Its Importance, Place and Potential* (Cambridge: Grove Books, R 9, 2002).
15. Scott A. Ellington, 'The Costly Loss of Testimony', *Journal of Pentecostal Theology* 16 (2000), pp. 48–59.
16. Grudem, *The Gift of Prophecy*. This work is based on his earlier study, *The Gift of Prophecy in 1 Corinthians* (Washington: University Press of America, 1982).
17. J.H. Ferguson, 'Prophecy', *Anglicans for Renewal* 28 (1987), p. 24.

5. The Sanctified Life

1. John Wesley, Sermon 85, 'On Working Out Our Own Salvation', Part 2, Section 1, in Jackson edn of Wesley's Works, 6:509, cited by Donald W. Dayton, *Theological Roots of Pentecostalism* (Peabody MA: Hendrickson, 2000, 1987), pp. 45–6.
2. Vinson Synan, *The Holiness-Pentecostal Tradition: Charismatic Movements in the Twentieth Century,* 2nd edn (Grand Rapids: Eerdmans, 1997) p. 6; cf. J.I. Packer, *Keep in Step with the Spirit* (Leicester: IVP, 1984), pp. 132–45; and Ian Randall, *What a Friend We Have in Jesus: The Evangelical Tradition* (London: Darton, Longman & Todd, 2005), pp. 115–19.
3. Synan, *The Holiness-Pentecostal Tradition,* p. 7.
4. *ibid.,* p. 9.
5. *ibid.,* pp. 12–13.
6. *ibid.,* pp. 26–7.
7. *ibid.,* p. 81.
8. Walter J. Hollenweger, *The Pentecostals: The Charismatic Movement in the Churches* (London: SCM, 1972), p. 50.
9. Randall, *What a Friend We Have,* pp. 119–24; Packer, *Keep in Step,* p. 146.
10. Packer, *Keep in Step,* p. 148.
11. *ibid.,* p. 148.
12. Hollenweger, *The Pentecostals,* pp. 23–5.
13. *ibid.,* pp. 399–412.
14. Edward D. O'Connor, *The Pentecostal Movement in the Catholic Church* (Notre Dame: Ave Maria Press, 1971), pp. 171–2.
15. Heribert Mühlen, *A Charismatic Theology: Initiation in the Spirit* (London: Burns & Oates, 1978), pp. 157–60.
16. This resonates with liberationist Pentecostals, e.g. Samuel Solivan, *The Spirit, Pathos and Liberation: Toward an Hispanic Pentecostal Theology* (Sheffield: Sheffield Academic Press, JPTSup 14, 1998).
17. Mühlen, *A Charismatic Theology,* p. 160.
18. René Laurentin, *Catholic Pentecostalism* (London: Darton, Longman and Todd, 1977), pp. 173–7.
19. *ibid.,* p. 174.
20. For a Pentecostal theological proposal in relation to social ethics, see Murray W. Dempster, 'The Structure of a Christian Ethic Informed by Pentecostal Experience: Soundings in the Moral Significance of Glossolalia', in Wonsuk Ma and Robert P. Menzies, *The Spirit and Spirituality: Essays in Honour of Russell P. Spittler* (London: T & T Clark, JPTSup 24, 2004), pp. 108–40.
21. William K. Kay, *Pentecostals in Britain* (Carlisle: Paternoster, 2000), pp. 154–88.
22. It is interesting that Nigel Scotland, *Charismatics and the Next Millennium: Do They Have a Future?* (London: Hodder & Stoughton,

1995), in an otherwise excellent book, offers no account of holiness as part of charismatic spirituality.

23. Anne E. Dyer, 'Holiness through the Twentieth Century', in William K. Kay and Anne E. Dyer, *Pentecostal and Charismatic Studies: A Reader* (London: SCM, 2004), pp. 127–31.

24. Simon Chan, *Pentecostal Theology and the Christian Spiritual Tradition* (Sheffield: Sheffield Academic Press, JPTSup 21, 2000).

25. Robin Parry, *Worshipping Trinity: Coming back to the heart of worship* (Milton Keynes: Paternoster, 2005).

26. Chan, *Pentecostal theology*, p. 64. However, note the problem observed by William W. and Robert P. Menzies, who state that the correlation of power with holiness can lead to claims to justify sinful behaviour on the basis of spiritual power, see William W. & Robert P. Menzies, *Spirit and Power: Foundation of Pentecostal Experience* (Grand Rapids: Zondervan, 2000), p. 204. I think Chan would agree that the problem exists, but that one should not separate them entirely.

27. *Ibid.*, p. 66.

28. Parry, *Worshipping Trinity*, p. 59.

29. *ibid.*, pp. 62–3.

6. Empowered Kingdom Witness

1. David Pytches, *Come, Holy Spirit: Learning How to Minister in the Power of the Holy Spirit* (London: Hodder & Stoughton, 1985), pp. 11–16; see also Nigel Scotland, *Charismatics and the Next Millennium: Do They Have a Future?* (London: Hodder & Stoughton, 1995), ch. 9.

2. Harvey Cox, *Fire from Heaven: The Rise of Pentecostal Spirituality and the Reshaping of Religion in the Twenty-First Century* (London: Cassell, 1996), ch. 5.

3. *ibid.*, pp. 99–100.

4. The accounts of Pentecostalism in non-Western contexts by major commentators demonstrate this, e.g. Walter J. Hollenweger, *Pentecostalism: Origins and Developments Worldwide* (Peabody MA: Hendrickson, 1997), chs. 5, 6, 7, 8 and 10; Cox, *Fire from Heaven*, chs. 9, 11 and 12; and Allan Anderson, *An Introduction to Pentecostalism* (Cambridge: Cambridge University Press, 2004), chs. 4, 6 and 7.

5. Hollenweger, *Pentecostalism*, pp. 243–5.

6. For a helpful discussion, see William W. Menzies, 'Reflections on Suffering: A Pentecostal Perspective', in Wonsuk Ma and Robert P. Menzies (eds.), *The Spirit and Spirituality: Essays in Honour of Russel P. Spittler* (London: T & T Clark, JPTSup 24, 2004), pp. 141–9.

7. For a discussion of this in relation to theologies of healing and the views of Pentecostals and charismatics, see Mark J. Cartledge,

Practical Theology: Charismatic and Empirical Perspectives (Carlisle: Paternoster, 2003), ch. 9.

8. See the discussion in T. Smail, A. Walker and N. Wright, *Charismatic Renewal: The Search for a Theology* (London: SPCK, 1993), pp. 73–5, 88–9.
9. See Max Turner, *Baptism in the Holy Spirit* (Cambridge: Grove Books, R 2, 2000) for a discussion of the exegetical issues.
10. Michael Harper, *Walk in the Spirit* (London: Hodder & Stoughton, 1968), p. 21.
11. For a discussion of the biblical and early historical material with a view to integrating baptism in the Spirit within Roman Catholic teaching, see Kilian McDonnell and George T. Montague, *Christian Initiation and Baptism in the Holy Spirit: Evidence from the First Eight Centuries* (Collegeville: The Liturgical Press, 1991).
12. Ian Randall, *What a Friend We Have in Jesus: The Evangelical Tradition* (London: Darton, Longman and Todd, 2005), chs. 2 and 9.
13. John Wimber with Kevin Springer, *Power Evangelism: Signs and Wonders Today* (London: Hodder & Stoughton, 1985).
14. For a critical and insightful sociological account, see Stephen Hunt, *Anyone for Alpha? Evangelism in a Post-Christian Society* (London: Darton, Longman and Todd, 2001); and for a more academic treatment see his *The Alpha Enterprise: Evangelism in a Post-Christian Era* (Aldershot: Ashgate, 2004).
15. E.g. see Ed Silvoso, *That None Should Perish: How to Reach Entire Cities for Christ Through Prayer Evangelism* (Ventura CA: Regal Books, 1994).
16. See Mark J. Cartledge, 'The Symbolism of Charismatic Glossolalia', *Journal of Empirical Theology* 12.1 (1999), pp. 37–51.
17. Margaret M. Poloma, 'Glossolalia, Liminality, and Empowered Kingdom Building: A Sociological Perspective' in Mark J. Cartledge (ed.), *Speaking in Tongues: Multi-disciplinary Perspectives* (Carlisle: Paternoster, 2006), ch. 6.
18. Andrew Lord, *Spirit-Shaped Mission: A Holistic Charismatic Missiology* (Carlisle: Paternoster, 2005).
19. John Leach, *Developing Prayer Ministry: A New Introduction for Churches* (Cambridge: Grove Books, R 1, 2000) p. 7; see also John Leach, *Person-Centred Prayer Ministry* (Cambridge: Grove Books, R 14, 2003).
20. Donald W. Dayton, *Theological Roots of Pentecostalism* (Peabody, MA: Hendrickson, 2000, 1987), pp. 19–23.
21. Peter Althouse, *Spirit of the Last Days: Pentecostal Eschatology in Conversation with Jürgen Moltmann* (London: T & T Clark, 2003), p. 18, who also notes its decline in use from 1948 because of a schismatic movement, p. 44.
22. Dayton, *Theological Roots*, pp. 26–8.
23. Althouse, *Spirit of the Last Days*, p. 20.

24. *ibid.*, p. 56, notes A. Walker, 'Thoroughly Modern: Sociological Reflections on the Charismatic Movement at the End of the Twentieth Century', in Stephen Hunt, Malcolm Hamilton and Tony Walter (eds.), *Charismatic Christianity: Sociological Perspectives* (Basingstoke: Macmillan, 1997), pp. 17–42 (p. 32).
25. Dayton, *Theological Roots*, p. 146.

7. The Community of Interpreters

1. See my summary of classical Pentecostal hermeneutics in 'Text-Community-Spirit: The Challenge of Pentecostal Theological Method to British Evangelicalism' in Steven Holmes (ed.), *British Evangelical Identities* (Milton Keynes: Paternoster, forthcoming).
2. Kenneth J. Archer, *A Pentecostal Hermeneutic for the Twenty-First Century: Spirit, Scripture and Community* (London: T & T Clark, JPTSup 28, 2004), pp. 72–91.
3. *ibid.*, p. 74.
4. *ibid.*, p. 97.
5. *ibid.*, pp. 100–3.
6. *ibid.*, p. 106.
7. J.C. Thomas, 'Reading the Bible from within Our Traditions: A Pentecostal Hermeneutic as Test Case', in J.B. Green and M. Turner (eds.), *Between Two Horizons: Spanning New Testament Studies and Systematic Theology* (Grand Rapids: Eerdmans, 2000), pp. 108–22. A fuller version can be found in J.C. Thomas, 'Women, Pentecostals and the Bible: An Experiment in Pentecostal Hermeneutics', *Journal of Pentecostal Theology* 5 (1994), pp. 41–56 (p. 50).
8. Archer, *A Pentecostal Hermeneutic*, ch. 6.
9. Aimee Semple McPherson, *This is That: Personal Experiences, Sermons and Writings* (Los Angeles, CA: Echo Park Evangelistic Association, 1923).
10. *ibid.*, p. 116.
11. *ibid.*, p. 379.
12. *ibid.*, pp. 770–9.
13. *ibid.*, p. 774.
14. *ibid.*, p. 774.
15. *ibid.*, p. 776.
16. *ibid.*, p. 777.
17. Mark Stibbe, *Times of Refreshing: A Practical Theology of Revival for Today* (London: Marshall Pickering, 1995), pp. 2–3.
18. *ibid.*, p. 5.
19. J. Lyon, 'The Fourth Wave and the Approaching Millennium: Some Problems with Charismatic Hermeneutics', *Anvil: An Anglican Evangelical Journal for Theology and Mission*, 15.3 (1998), pp. 169–80 (p. 172).

20. Mark Stibbe, 'This is That: Some Thoughts Concerning Charismatic Hermeneutics', *Anvil: An Anglican Evangelical Journal for Theology and Mission* 15.3 (1998), pp. 181–93.

Conclusion

1. As far as I am aware, the first person to use this metaphor in relation to charismatic spirituality is Mark Bonnington, lecturer in New Testament studies at St John's College, Durham.
2. George A. Maloney (tr.), *Hymns of Divine Love by St Symeon the New Theologian* (Denville, NJ: Dimension Books, 1976), p. 9.

SELECT BIBLIOGRAPHY

Albrecht, Daniel E. *Rites in the Spirit: A Ritual Approach to Pentecostal / Charismatic Spirituality,* Sheffield Academic Press, JPTS 17, 1999

Allen, David. *The Unfailing Stream: A Charismatic Church History in Outline,* Tonbridge, Sovereign World, 1994

Anderson, Allan. *An Introduction to Pentecostalism: Global Charismatic Christianity,* Cambridge, Cambridge University Press, 2004

Archer, Kenneth J. *A Pentecostal Hermeneutic for the Twenty-First Century: Spirit, Scripture and Community,* London, T & T Clark, JPTSup 28, 2004

Burgess, Stanley M. *The Holy Spirit: Ancient Christian Traditions,* Peabody MA, Hendrickson, 1984

—— *The Holy Spirit: Eastern Christian Traditions,* 2nd edn, Peabody, MA, Hendrickson, 1993

—— *The Holy Spirit: Medieval Roman Catholic and Reformation Traditions,* Peabody, MA, Hendrickson, 1997

Burgess Stanley M., and Eduard M. Van der Mass (eds.). *The New International Dictionary of Pentecostal and Charismatic Movements – Revised and Expanded Edition,* Grand Rapids, Zondervan, 2002

Cartledge, Mark J. *Practical Theology: Charismatic and Empirical Perspectives,* Carlisle, Paternoster, 2003

—— *The Gift of Speaking in Tongues: The Holy Spirit, the Human Spirit and the Gift of Holy Speech,* Cambridge, Grove Books, R 19, 2005

Chan, Simon. *Pentecostal Theology and the Christian Spiritual Tradition,* Sheffield, Sheffield Academic Press, JPTS 21, 2000

Cox, Harvey. *Fire From Heaven: The Rise of Pentecostal Spirituality and the Reshaping of Religion in the Twenty-First Century,* London, Cassell, 1996

Dayton, Donald W. *Theological Roots of Pentecostalism,* Peabody MA, Hendrickson, 2000, 1987

Goldingay, John. 'Charismatic Spirituality: Some Theological Reflections', *Theology* 789 (1996), pp. 178–87

Grudem, Wayne. *The Gift of Prophecy,* Eastbourne, Kingsway, 1988

Hilborn, David (ed.). *'Toronto' in Perspective: Papers on the New Charismatic Wave of the Mid 1990s,* Carlisle, Evangelical Alliance/ Paternoster, 2001

Hocken, Peter. *Streams of Renewal: The Origins and Early Development of the Charismatic Movement in Great Britain,* 2nd edn, Carlisle, Paternoster, 1997

Hollenweger, Walter J. *The Pentecostals: The Charismatic Movement in the Churches,* London, SCM, 1972

  Pentecostalism: Origins and Developments Worldwide, Peabody MA, Hendrickson, 1997

Kay, William K. *Pentecostals in Britain,* Carlisle, Paternoster, 2000

Kay, William K., and Anne E. Dyer (eds.). *Pentecostal and Charismatic Studies: A Reader,* London, SCM, 2004

Laurentin, René. *Catholic Pentecostalism,* London, Darton, Longman & Todd, 1977

Lord, Andrew. *Spirit-Shaped Mission: A Holistic Charismatic Missiology,* Carlisle, Paternoster, 2005

Ma, Wonsuk and Robert P. Menzies (eds.). *The Spirit and Spirituality: Essays in Honour of Russell P. Spittler,* London, T & T Clark, JPTSup 24, 2004

McDonnell, Kilian and George T. Montague, *Christian Initiation and Baptism in the Holy Spirit: Evidence from the First Eight Centuries,* Collegeville, The Liturgical Press, 1991

Mühlen, Heribert. *A Charismatic Theology: Initiation in the Spirit,* London, Burns & Oates, 1978

O'Connor, Edward D. *The Pentecostal Movement in the Catholic Church,* Notre Dame, Ave Maria Press, 1971

Menzies, William W. and Robert P. *Spirit and Power: Foundations of Pentecostal Experience*, Grand Rapids, Zondervan, 2000

Packer, James I. *Keep in Step with the Spirit,* Leicester, IVP, 1984

Pytches, David. *Come, Holy Spirit: Learning How to Minister in the Power of the Holy Spirit*, London, Hodder & Stoughton, 1985

Scotland, Nigel. *Charismatics and the Next Millennium: Do They Have a Future?* London, Hodder & Stoughton, 1995

Smail, Thomas, Andrew Walker and Nigel Wright, *Charismatic Renewal: The Search for a Theology,* London, SPCK, 1993

Solivan, Samuel. *The Spirit, Pathos and Liberation: Toward an Hispanic Pentecostal Theology,* Sheffield, Sheffield Academic Press, JPTSup 14, 1998

Steven, James H.S. *Worship in the Spirit: Charismatic Worship in the Church of England,* Carlisle, Paternoster, 2002

Stibbe, Mark. *Times of Refreshing: A Practical Theology of Revival for Today,* London, Marshall Pickering, 1995

Suurmond, Jean-Jacques. *Word and Spirit at Play: Towards a Charismatic Theology,* London, SCM, 1994

Synan, Vinson. *The Holiness-Pentecostal Tradition: Charismatic Movements in the Twentieth Century,* 2nd edn, Grand Rapids, Eerdmans, 1997

Turner, Max. *The Holy Spirit and Spiritual Gifts: Then and Now*, Carlisle, Paternoster, 1996

Warrington, K. (ed.). *Pentecostal Perspectives,* Carlisle, Paternoster, 1998

Wimber, John with Kevin Springer, *Power Evangelism: Signs and Wonders Today,* London, Hodder & Stoughton, 1985

—— *Power Healing*, London, Hodder & Stoughton, 1986